T0311394

PHILOSOPHY OF TIME

THE BASICS

What is time? Does it pass? Is the future open? Why do we care? *Philosophy of Time: The Basics* doesn't answer these questions. It does give you an opinionated introduction to thinking a bit more deeply about them. Written in a way that assumes no philosophical background from its readers, this book looks at central topics in philosophy of time and shows how they relate to other time-related topics – from theoretical physics (without the maths!) to your own mortality. Additional questions include:

- In what way is time different to space?
- How long is the present?
- Does the Theory of Relativity show time doesn't pass?
- What makes time have a direction or 'arrow'?
- Can you be harmed by your own death?

Allowing the reader to think more deeply about time, this book begins to untangle some of the most difficult knots in all of philosophy. It also provides practical advice to prospective time-travelers.

Graeme A. Forbes has been working on philosophy of time for over a decade. He was Lecturer in Philosophy at the University of Kent before going freelance in 2022. He remains an Honorary Senior Lecturer at the University of Kent.

The Basics Series

The Basics is a highly successful series of accessible guidebooks which provide an overview of the fundamental principles of a subject area in a jargon-free and undaunting format.

Intended for students approaching a subject for the first time, the books both introduce the essentials of a subject and provide an ideal springboard for further study. With over 50 titles spanning subjects from artificial intelligence (AI) to women's studies, *The Basics* are an ideal starting point for students seeking to understand a subject area.

Each text comes with recommendations for further study and gradually introduces the complexities and nuances within a subject.

For a full list of titles in this series, please visit
www.routledge.com/The-Basics/book-series/B

PHILOSOPHY OF TIME

THE BASICS

Graeme A. Forbes

Routledge
Taylor & Francis Group

NEW YORK AND LONDON

Designed cover image: © Getty Images

First published 2024
by Routledge
605 Third Avenue, New York, NY 10158

and by Routledge
4 Park Square, Milton Park, Abingdon, Oxon, OX14 4RN

Routledge is an imprint of the Taylor & Francis Group, an informa business

© 2024 Graeme A. Forbes

ISBN: 978-1-032-03869-8 (hbk)
ISBN: 978-1-032-03868-1 (pbk)
ISBN: 978-1-003-18945-9 (ebk)

DOI: 10.4324/9781003189459

Typeset in Bembo
by KnowledgeWorks Global Ltd.

CONTENTS

PREFACE

Time, it has been said, is the hardest knot in all of philosophy. This book will not succeed in unpicking it, but will draw your attention to a number of the particularly difficult threads. We are creatures in time and of time; we can't really make sense of the world without experiencing it over time. Nonetheless, since the very earliest philosophers there has been a tug-of-war over the question of whether time is anything more than an artefact of our thought. Through the course of this book, we will examine whether time passes, whether experience gives us reasons to think it does, whether there is a unique present time, how long it lasts, and whether we last through change in what time is present. We will examine whether time has a direction, whether the past and the future are settled, and whether they can change. We will think about how time matters in our decision making, in our records of what happened, and in our evaluations of how our life is going. One of the reasons the philosophy of time is so knotty is that there are so many problems bound together; problems, in many cases, it seems almost absurd to ask; how can there be a debate about whether time passes that has *lasted over 2500 years!*? Another reason that we tie ourselves in knots about these issues is because they affect how we live. As English Poet T.S. Eliot wrote:

> But only in time can the moment in the rose-garden,
> The moment in the arbour where the rain beat,
> The moment in the draughty church at smokefall
> Be remembered; involving past and future.
> Only through time is time conquered.[1]

Our unpicking of time takes place within time and all of the things we do and value are bound up within that tangle.

This book is about the philosophy of time. More specifically, it covers three themes: the passage of time, the differences between past and future, and some philosophical problems of living in time. It is aimed as an introduction to the philosophy of time. No background in philosophy is assumed, and technical work is avoided where possible. Given that the book involves some discussion of theoretical physics, it's not possible to remove all technical detail, but the aim throughout has been to give a sense of the puzzles, rather than to give the last word on them.

This is an opinionated introduction: I have not tried to hide my personality or my views from the reader. My opinions come through in a number of ways. Firstly, in the choice of topics. Many introductions to the philosophy of time focus entirely on issues in metaphysics and perhaps the philosophy of physics: I have deliberately included topics such as the philosophy of history, because I think they *ought* to be the concern of philosophers of time, even if historically they haven't been.

My opinions come through also in the philosophical approach. I take it one of the goals of philosophy is to unify our scientific account of the world with our lived experience of it. But some philosophers feel that the scientific account of the world and the practice of living it are entirely separate projects that should be treated separately. On the contrary, I don't think either science or life can be understood separately from the other.

My opinions come through in the framework I presuppose. I am a philosopher in a particular time and place of a particular age with a particular history. This can't help but be revealed in my writing. I am an analytic philosopher writing in the English language, although I bring in influences outside that tradition, the dominant approach is from a particular strain of the analytic tradition that takes philosophy to be neither a matter of analysing our concepts nor deferring to science, but to, as clearly as possible, make sense of things.

Finally, my personality will come through in my sense of humour. I occasionally use the notes to make comments for my own amusement. The humour varies in subtlety but has a serious conviction behind it. Making sense of things is one of the most valuable things you could do with your time. Why not enjoy it? It is a cruel mistake to confuse taking philosophy seriously with thinking that something is intellectually valuable only when it is conducted in a sombre way. Time is passing! Enjoy yourself when you can!

This book was written during a time of transition in my life, and there are a few people I need to acknowledge. Thanks to Ray Briggs, David Corfield, Dorothy Lehane, and Ann C. Thresher for long-standing friendship and comments on various parts of the draft and to Andrew Beck,Marc Stratton, and Kristina Wischenkamper from Routledge for their patience. Chapters 5, 6, and 9 are especially indebted to the work of Tim Maudlin, David Z. Albert, and Mark Day (respectively), whose approaches have been very influential in my own framing of the issues. Much of this book is indebted to a longer monograph yet to be published, so I owe thanks to the many people who helped with the research on that project that allowed me to write this more introductory book. Finally, thanks to my students over the years at the University of Kent, particularly those who took my *Introduction to Philosophy of Time* module, for their love of wisdom.

NOTE

1 (1944:16)

THE PROBLEM OF CHANGE

Of the puzzles about time that we contend with, there is one that appears to be at the centre: the problem of change. If we want to understand time, we must understand change. What is change, and how do we get some?

One view is that change is just things being different at different times. Here are some different times:

551 BCE	1687	2022	2776	4476

Change, on this view, is just different things being the case at different locations on that timeline. But look at the timeline. It – *the timeline* – isn't changing! Change on this view, is just a matter of things being one way *at* a time and another way *at* another time. We can call this the '**at–at' theory of change**.

The idea here is that time is just a dimension along which things vary. Just as a flower bed can vary from having daffodils at one and to having tulips at the other, time can vary from having triremes anchoring in the Mediterranean at one period to having spaceships landing in the Sea of Tranquillity at another. The talk of things being 'located at a time' sounds a little artificial, but almost everyone agrees that time does vary with things being different at different times.

Some people think there is *more* to time than this. Variation along a dimension is nothing special. The electromagnetic spectrum varies from having X-rays at one frequency to radio waves at another.

DOI: 10.4324/9781003189459-1

Water varies from being ice at one pressure–temperature combination, to being steam at another. Variation along a dimension doesn't tell us anything about why time might be particularly philosophically interesting. If you think all change *is* is variation along a temporal dimension, the problem then is to explain why time seems so philosophically interesting. If you think there is more to time than variation along a temporal dimension, then the aim is to explain *what more there is* to time than the at–at view provides.

How do we get more than temporal variation into our account of change? It can't simply be a question of adding an extra ingredient, such as 'dynamism'! If we just said it's variation along a dimension plus *somethingsomethingsomething*, we would need to know why that extra-ingredient gave rise to change in combination with temporal variation. And we would also need to know why this extra ingredient wasn't just change with a different name. There's a danger of leaving change as utterly mysterious. It's one thing for change to be unexplainable in terms of other things. But if change isn't just variation along a temporal dimension, we need something positive to say about what it is. This is not just because it will make an explanation more satisfying if it has some content to it, but because it will allow us to establish *what we're talking about* in the first place.

I think change probably *is* going to end up being pretty mysterious. The rest of this chapter will be looking at various reasons why. Early twentieth-century Cambridge philosopher C.D. Broad described change as time's 'rock bottom peculiarity'.[1]

THE CONTRAST WITH SPACE

Even though change is going to be mysterious, I think we can get some grip on it. One thing we can do to fix what we mean by change is point to the contrast with space. Whatever time is, it's not the same as space. Even if we view them as fundamentally interrelated in a four-dimensional arrangement called 'space–time' (as we will in chapter 5), the time-like direction of space–time is different from the space-like directions. Another thing we can do is appeal to metaphor. Metaphors don't allow us to analyse something in terms of something else, but they allow us to draw our attention to similarities that among other things, can be useful for having understanding of things we otherwise couldn't express.

Metaphors of time as a river occur in Ancient Greek, Ancient Indian and Classical Chinese philosophical traditions. In the contemporary philosophical literature, we say time 'flows' or 'passes'; these have become the technical terms for the view that change in what time it is involves more than mere temporal variation. These metaphors of flow or passage draw our attention to the ways in which time contrasts with space. When we look at a timeline, with dates spread out along it, there is no flow or passage, just a series of unchanging relations between different times. The alternative to the at–at view is that there is a contrast between time and space such that change over time has no spatial equivalent. Variation across space is not change, and changes of what time it is are not simply variations along a temporal dimension.

I am going to call change over time that has no spatial equivalent **McTchange** (the 'T' is pronounced). It's much quicker than writing 'change in the sense McTaggart meant' over and over again. McTchange is named after the early twentieth-century Cambridge philosopher John McTaggart Ellis McTaggart. He was influential in insisting that change, if there was any, was not simply variation relative to times.

The at–at view denies that there is any McTchange, and a commitment to McTchange involves thinking that there is something more than the at–at view admits. But that doesn't exhaust the options. We could think that there's *less* than the at–at view admits. We can call such a view an '**error theory**' of change. An error theory might claim that there is no change, or that we are radically wrong about what change is. McTaggart himself thought that the at–at view wasn't enough for change, and that McTchange led to a contradiction, so he denied that there was any change. We're going to look at his argument in section 3. More recently Baron, Miller, and Tallant (2022) have defended a version of the error theory.

Both the at–at view and McTchange tend to be motivated by experiences of things (including ourselves) changing; they just disagree about how we should understand change. Of course, if you defend the view that change, in order to *count* as change, must be McTchange, you will describe the at–at view as denying that there is any change. But that doesn't make the at–at view an error theory of change, because even if it is not the correct account of change, it takes at face value our experience of things changing and attempts to provide an explanation of that. The debate becomes one about which explanation best makes sense of things, rather than whether we accept that we experience things changing.

If both the at–at view and McTchange agree that things change, why is it such a major issue? Who cares which of these accounts of change we go with? If this is a central concern of philosophy of time, it had better be clear why it matters. Change is fundamental to our description of various phenomena, from the role of time in theoretical physics, through biology, economics, history and working out if, right now, you are happy.

The main consequence this debate will have for discussions in other areas is by getting us to think about situated perspectives. If we treat a time as the present, we can make sense of how things are for someone at that time. But the debate about change forces us to ask whether that is just one time amongst others, each giving its occupants a perspective on the world, or whether there is change in the world pushing or pulling us from one time to another. Is time just a dimension of perspectives, or does it involve a *succession* of perspectives? As we shall see changing how we understand change affects how we think about issues in a range of other areas. These include the relationship between our perspectival experience of the world and science, and also questions about whether we can be responsible for our actions.

DYNAMIC VERSUS STATIC

The problem of change, as we set it up, involved two ways of understanding what change is. The first was 'at–at' change, where change is just variation along a temporal dimension. The second was McTchange, where change has no spatial equivalent. These two views of change give rise to two different views of what time is. If change is 'at–at' change, time is **static**. Some defenders of this view object to the term 'static' as it suggests that something is missing from such a view. As defenders of the view they don't think anything is missing. What's missing, if there is anything, is McTchange. If change is McTchange, time is **dynamic**. Error theories of change, in which it is claimed that there is no change, produce error theories of time. So, on this way of framing things, the central dispute in the philosophy of time is whether time is dynamic or static. Broadly speaking most contemporary physicists treat time as static, and most people who are not physicists think of time as dynamic.[2] This sets us up for a clash between common-sense and science.[3]

TENSED/TENSELESS TIME

You may find, in further reading about the philosophy of time, that the terms 'static' and 'dynamic' don't come up, but different terminology gets used:

Dynamic	Static
A-theory	B-theory (also C-theory)
Tensed	Tenseless

These are all different ways of making basically the same distinction, though sometimes they are used in a slightly different way. The tensed/tenseless distinction comes from a debate about whether language can get rid of 'tense' or not.[4] **Tense** is a feature of language that locates events in time relative to a present time. We can't make sense of English without tense; saying that an event is in 5 minutes communicates something very different than simply specifying the time the clock will say at the start of the event. If I don't know what the clock says now, knowing what time the clock will say when the event is due to begin won't make me leap out of my chair and start rushing to the event! The relation of an event to *now* is really important. But it became clear that the philosophical issue of the reality of time passing could not be settled by an appeal to how English works. For one thing, there are lots of other languages that work very differently: Some West African languages, like Yoruba, lack grammatical tense, but use other features of language (such as aspect) to convey what time something is happening at. The question is really whether the location of an event relative to *now* was required to describe the world accurately (perhaps using the kind of formal language that gets used in the study of logic, or by physicists). Time is tensed if our technical language for describing the world requires us to specify how things relate to the present moment. Time is tenseless if we can dispense with the present moment and just use dates to describe the conditions under which sentences are true or false. **Dates** specify time relationships in terms of the relations before, after, and simultaneous with. In this sense of 'date', 2.37pm and 16.2 seconds on a particular day counts as a date. When describing the world, if you can do everything with dates, there is no need for tenses.

A/B/C THEORY

The A/B theory distinction is very similar to the tense/tenseless distinction, but with the added complication that there's a third option: C-theory. McTaggart introduced a distinction between three ways of ordering different moments into series. The **A-series** is a series of events based on their relation to the present. At one end is the distant past, and then the near past, the present – this very moment! – and then the near future, and then the distant future. That is, the A-series is a series ordered by tense.

The B-series is a series ordered in terms of relations of before and after. This series might start with the Big Bang, and go through the billions of years until the solar system forms, life develops, computers are invented, I write this sentence, (13.8 billion years after the Big Bang), you read the sentence (after I have written it), the human race dies, the earth is engulfed by the sun, and the heat death of the universe occurs (after you have read it). That is, the B-series is ordered by dates. The B-series is the same moments as the A-series in the same order, but the basis of the ordering doesn't involve tense, just dates.

What about the **C-series**? Well, both the A-series and the B-series appeal to concepts of time to generate the ordering. Tenses require a *now*, an objective present. Dates require relations of earlier and later; before and after in time. The C-series has an ordering that doesn't involve any appeal to time. So, if there were some physical properties that varied from one end of the universe to the other, we could order a series by that, rather than by either dates or tense. And it looks like there is a physical property that varies from one end of the universe to the other! **Entropy** is a physical measure of disorder that was at its minimum in the Big Bang and will be at its maximum at the heat death of the universe. We could use a measure like entropy to come up with a C-series to order 'moments' in the same order as the A-series and the B-series, but without needing any time concepts whatsoever.

That's the A-series, the B-series, and the C-series. What about A-*theory*, B-*theory*, and C-*theory*? McTaggart thought that you needed all three series to explain time. You could only get relations of before and after, he thought, by applying the A-series to the things ordered by the C series. He also thought that the A-series was contradictory.

So **A-theory** is the view that we need an objective present to make sense of time, and **B-theory** is the view that we can make sense of time with relations of before and after, but no objective present time. **C-theory** is the view that time doesn't require an objective present, or a fundamental distinction between earlier and later; both are imposed by our perspective on the world. Sometimes C-theory is treated as a special case of B-theory (since they are united by their denial of an objective present), and sometimes it looks like it is an error theory (since we are wrong to think that the universe contains time of either variety). In chapter 6, we'll be thinking about the role of earlier/later relations and physics in a little more detail.

I'm going to stick with 'dynamic' and 'static' as my labels for the debate about whether time passes or not, because I think framing it in terms of an objective present is unhelpful, and the A/B terminology forces us to explain McTaggart's views just so we understand the name of the view. But in chapter 2, we'll be thinking about some of the problems of thinking that there is an objective present moment. I think that in some situations, the two questions of whether there is an objective present and whether there is change that is not mere temporal variation can be answered differently. When those situations come up, I'll try to mention it.

Now that we've got the distinction between dynamic and static views of time, we can get into the big philosophical question that it gives rise to: is a dynamic view coherent?

McTAGGART'S INFAMOUS ARGUMENT FOR THE UNREALITY OF TIME

The worry about whether dynamic views are coherent is expressed in a number of ways. Sometimes these expressions look like reformulations of the same idea. Sometimes they look like different arguments with similar conclusions. We'll start with the most famous, before moving on to more recent ones. McTaggart, as we have seen, did much to set up the contemporary debate. But he also argued that change was impossible, and so time was unreal. Let's look at his infamous argument for the unreality of time.

The thrust of McTaggart's argument is that McTchange commits you to a contradiction: e.g. that it is, objectively, both Monday and Tuesday. To put this another way, suppose you think that both Monday and Tuesday exist, and you think one of them is objectively present – not merely present-for-me but the uniquely present moment of time. Either Monday *was* present and Tuesday *is* present, or Monday *is* present and Tuesday *will be* present. But, McTaggart thinks, to add 'was' and 'will be' here is just to say 'Yesterday Monday *is* present' or 'Tomorrow Tuesday *is* present'. 'Yesterday Monday *is* present' and 'Tuesday *is* present' contradict each other, since the present is supposed to be unique.

Here's a reconstruction of McTaggart's argument:

McT1   For time to be real there must be McTChange.
McT2   For McTChange to be real, every event (except the first and last) must be past, present, and future.
McT3   No event may be past and present, or past and future, or present and future.
McT4   If every event must be past, present, and future and no event may be past and present, or past and future, or present and future, McTChange cannot be real.

therefore

McTC   Time is not real.

Almost everyone accepts that McTaggart's argument doesn't show that time is not real. They just disagree on how bad the argument it is.

One response says that the argument doesn't show time isn't real, but shows us how difficult philosophy of time is:

> McTaggart's argument is fallacious, but it is fallacious in such a deep and basic way that an adequate answer to it must supply a rather extensive analysis of the concept of time, along with a host of neighbouring concepts.

> (Gale 1968:65)

Another response thinks that it's just based on a mistake:

> To sum up. I believe that McTaggart's main argument against the reality of Time is a philosophical howler.
>
> (Broad 1938:316)

I tend to side with those who think the argument is fairly easy to reject. But here's a problem. Lots of *really clever* people, who have thought about it a lot, think there's something going on, something that I can't see. For me, the biggest challenge with McTaggart's argument is working out why people find it convincing.

It would be very easy to be dismissive of McTaggart's argument. One of the reasons to be cautious about being so dismissive is that McTaggart seems to have anticipated the most tempting response. There is no contradiction in things being past *and* present, or present *and* future, because they are past, present, and future *at different times*. McTaggart thinks that this response doesn't help, because each of those times must themselves change from being future to present to past.

That is, the idea of drawing a bunch of timelines, each of which providing an A-series that orders everything in terms of whether it is past, present, or future isn't going to give us McTchange. It's just going to give a bunch of different timelines that vary in what properties they have at different locations. The passage of time can't simply be variation of presentness according to different A series, because change was meant to be something that we can't understand in terms of mere variation. Drawing more timelines didn't give us change, just another dimension of variation. No matter how many dimensions of variation we have, that won't be enough to give us McTchange, rather than something compatible with the 'at–at' view.

PHILOSOPHY OF TIME AFTER McTAGGART

Many people have taken McTaggart's argument to set the agenda for philosophy of time. Different responses to the argument have become starting points for many different positions.

One useful thing about the reconstruction of McTaggart's argument (above) is it allows us to see which responses are available. You can reject one or more of the premises (McT1–3).

If you reject McT1, you simply deny that time passes in a way that space does not. Variation across time is no different to variation across space, though it might be that time has an earlier–later ordering that space does not. If you accept this response, you defend a static view of time.

If you reject McT2 you deny that events are both past and present, or present and future, or future and past. Note that the argument doesn't need to claim that *every* event is past, present, and future (except the first and last). Just having a single event that had more than one of those properties would be enough. If you accept there is change but that events never have more than one of these properties, it might be because you think that events are only ever present; they never become past events. The problem with this view is that you've been to lots of past events. Sure, they were present at the time, but what are we talking about if we can't say *of them* that they are now past?

If you reject McT3 you deny the claim that an event being past and present, or present and future, or future and past are incompatible. It's only incompatible if they are more than one of those *at the same time*.

Remember that McTaggart anticipates that objection! Sometimes people who reject McT3 appeal to extra time dimensions at which there is no contradiction, but McTaggart would respond that it's contradictory for all of those timelines to accurately describe reality. A more common solution is to say that there is no contradiction because there is McTchange in what properties things have. But McTaggart thinks this doesn't help, because you haven't yet shown that McTchange is coherent.

I think that what McTaggart's argument shows is that you can't explain McTchange in non-McTchanging terms. To say that something is present and then past bakes McTchange into the 'and then'. McTaggart will object that that's where the problem lies, but it looks like it's just a feature rather than a problem. I basically think David H. Sandford (1968:373) gets the diagnosis right:

> McTaggart's argument is a *reductio ad absurdum:* a contradiction follows from the assumption there is an A series. The same assumption from which a contradiction is said to follow surely cannot be disallowed in the attempt to show that it really does not follow.

A *reductio ad absurdum* [literally: reduction to absurdity] argument is one where you grant an assumption, and then show that unacceptable consequences arise from accepting it. Sanford argues that when we accept McT1, we are allowed to appeal to change in what time it is to avoid a time being present and then past creating an incompatibility. McT3 is only a problem if we are not already allowed to appeal to McTchange. But we are allowed to appeal to McTchange, Sanford says. We started off by assuming that things McTchange.

The question about change remains whether McTchange is coherent. Is there something contradictory or theoretically suspect about it, or is it just a basic concept that cannot be explained in terms of other things? (One might opt for the third view that it is coherent, but nothing McTchanges. We'll set that to one side here.) But McTaggart's argument was not the only attack on the coherence of McTchange. As we shall see, various other attacks have been made, many of which claim to be different versions of McTaggart's argument.

RATES

If time passes, how fast does it do so? Here are two answers:

- It does pass: at a rate of 1 second per second.
- It doesn't make any sense to ask at what rate time passes, because it doesn't pass relative to anything.

The question has been put forward by many philosophers as a *reductio ad absurdum* of McTchange:

R1: We assume that there is a special change that takes place when time passes: McTchange.

R2: As a type of change, McTchange must have a rate at which it McTchanges.

R3: McTchange doesn't have a rate at which it McTchanges (1 second/second doesn't count!)

RC: There is no McTchange.

If we assume time passes, we are left with an absurd conclusion; that there is a change that has no rate.

Let's think about our two answers again.

What's wrong with thinking that there is a rate of 1 second per second? Eric Olson (2009:5) argues that 1 second per second isn't a possible rate, because the seconds cancel each other out. We just get a rate of 1, which is a number. There is some debate about whether this is a problem.[5] We can think of rates where the two numbers are the same. In the end, the mortality rate of humans is 1. For every human who lives, eventually, you have a human who dies. That's a mortality rate of 1 human per human. It's not clear that there's a conceptual difficulty here.

The problem seems to be that it's missing the force of the question. The point is that McTchange is meant to be a change with no spatial equivalent. So we need to explain the sense in which time passes at a rate of 1 second per second, but space doesn't 'pass' at a rate of 1 metre per metre. Pointing out that seconds last a second, and metres are a metre long doesn't capture the difference. This is why some, like C.D. Broad (1959) argue that the question makes no sense. He rejects R2. He argues that McTchange is a change *of* time, not a change *in* time. Only changes in time need rates.

Eric Olson (2009) argues that claiming that McTchange is a special kind of change that has no rate risks making McTchange mysterious. If McTchange is a change unlike any other, in that it lacks a rate, how can we understand what it is? As with McTaggart's argument, we seem forced into the view that McTchange can't be explained in terms of anything else.

THE 'WHEN AM I?' PROBLEM

So far, we have been thinking about the question of whether or not there is McTchange, in order to settle whether we should have a static or a dynamic view of time. But dynamic views come in different varieties. As we saw in response to McTaggart's argument, some people deny that there are any times that aren't present. This view is called **Presentism**.[6] The idea of Presentism seems to be that we only ever experience things as present, so we should treat only present things as being real. One argument, developed independently by Craig Bourne (2002, 2006) and David Braddon-Mitchell (2004), tries to show that there's a problem with dynamic views that aren't Presentism.

There are a number of non-Presentist dynamic views. Here's a brief summary of them.

The Growing Block view is committed to the past existing and the future not existing.[7] The idea is that reality gets bigger as things happen.

The Moving Spotlight view is committed to the past present and future all being equally real, but the present is picked out as special in some way, as though there were a spotlight on it that moves as the present gets later and later.[8] The idea here is that presentness is not a matter of existence or being more real, but of having some other property.

The Shrinking Tree view also treats the past present future as being equally real, but accepts that there are many, equally real, futures, representing different ways things could go.[9] As those possible futures cease to be possible, they drop out of existence. You can represent this as a tree-like structure, with the past as a trunk, and the future as a branching structure fanning out from the trunk. The present is the earliest point at which branching occurs.

The Shrinking Block view treats the future as existing and the past as not existing.[10] It is the mirror-image of the Growing Block view. The idea seems to be that all our evidence lies in the future, so we should accord existence to the things that we can potentially see and touch, rather than the things lost to the past.

When I talk of 'the past' existing, or 'the future' existing, this is perhaps a little misleading. We needn't think of them as large objects, such as regions of space–time. They could be collections of things – tables, football matches, lightning strikes – that are located earlier than the present (i.e. in the past) or later than the present (i.e. in the future). The past is just the collection of all the things that are located earlier than now. Wait, I mean *now*. No; *NOW!* (Etc.)

The 'When Am I?' problem takes people located at non-present times, and asks if they think they are present. If they do, we then ask what their evidence is that they are present. If their evidence that they are present is the same as our evidence that we are present, our evidence for our presentness can't count for much. We only have good evidence that we are present if that evidence would be different if we were not present, the thought goes. Imagine some historical figure, Mary Queen of Scots for example, located in the 16th century, wondering if she is present. She is not wondering merely whether she is at the time she is at, but whether that time is the objectively special present one. If she is even *capable* of thinking this then we have a problem. We have a problem because it undermines our evidence that we are present. Why should we be so confident we're at the *special* time, when there she is being fooled by the same kind of evidence that we rely on! So our confidence in being present is undermined. But worse than that, we have reason to believe we are *not* present. Statistically, given how many more times are past than are present, we should be much more confident we are at a past one rather than a present one.

The problem gets going because there seem to be two different uses of 'is present' in play. One is where something is present when it is at the same time as us. For example, I think the time I am writing this at is present, and you think the time you are reading it is present.[11] Since we're both located at different times, we are calling different times present. This is the same as using 'here' to refer to different places, and 'I' to refer to different people. 'Here' picks out the place the speaker is, and 'I' picks out the person the speaker is. The other way of using 'is present' is where we pick out a time as being the unique time whether things have stopped being future but are not yet past. So we have a sense in which every time can be said to be present at itself (just as every place can be said to be here at itself) that is in tension with a sense in which at most one time is really present. Given that we normally treat the time that we are at as being present, if we accept that there are multiple times, we have no reason to think the time we are at is unique in being the present one. No evidence, that is, in the absence of some further story besides that we are at the time.

Philosophers have responded to this problem in a couple of different ways. One response is to argue that the statement of the problem runs into difficulties.[12] One form this takes is to say that we cannot step outside some particular time of assessment and ask what is objectively present. As soon as we are speaking relative to some time, that time will be the uniquely present one. If we are assessing the claim that Mary Queen of Scots is present from a time at which she was alive, then it's true that she is present. This response may be slightly unsatisfactory, since it could equally apply to 'here' or 'I'. It doesn't seem to address the thought that 'now' is meant to point out an objective present, in a way neither 'here' or 'I' do.[13]

Another response is that Mary Queen of Scots doesn't have the same evidence as us that she is present when she is past, because she doesn't have any evidence *at all*. People are only in a position to say that they are present when they are at the objective present, because it's only when they are objectively present that the conditions are right. One version of this response is that it's not enough to pay attention to the location in time of Mary Queen of Scots, but also to her activities. It's not true, the response goes, that she's located in the past *thinking* that she's present, because the thoughts are 'perfective' (i.e. finished). That is, it's not that she is thinking she is present, but that she *thought* she *was* present. When she was thinking she was right, but just as she is no longer present, neither is her thinking.[14]

Kristie Miller (2018) argues that this response faces a problem: in claiming that the past exists, the motivation was to say that the past is like the present (so we can offer a unified treatment of the past and present). But to make the kind of distinction between present thinking and past having thought required, we need a disunified treatment of past and present. Why say the past and present both exist, if past existence is totally unlike present existence? Certainly, this response relies on thinking that the past is in some ways like the present (there's a way it is that outruns how we think about it) but in some ways unlike the present (nothing is happening there). The question is whether that combination of similarity and difference is a problem.

THE FROZEN PRESENT

Whereas the 'When Am I?' problem focusses on what makes the present different to other times, the Frozen Present problem challenges the defender of the dynamic view to explain what the passage of time *is*.

Kit Fine (2005) provides the challenge by asking us to consider a complete description of reality. This description tells us about all the things that there are, and all the ways that they are. Additionally, it tells us which time is the objectively uniquely present one.

Even if we had *all that* information, we would still have nothing that told us that the view we were considering was dynamic. That complete description would be perfectly compatible with a world where the present was *frozen*. In such a world, there is a unique time that is objectively present, but which time that is never changes.

In fact, it looks like *no* description you could give of the world at a single moment in time will show that the world is dynamic. Even if the description told us that the world was dynamic, we wouldn't actually be able to point to any instance of McTchange, we would just have the claim that the world features some. This might not be a problem for a dynamic view. It may just show us that we can't describe the world by explaining what there is and how it is at a single moment of time. Fine takes it to show that there is a problem from what he calls 'standard realism' about tense.

If a *complete* description of the world doesn't include McTchange on the standard account, Fine argues we should adopt a 'non-standard' account. He suggests two non-standard accounts of time.

Relativism is the view that the facts that make up reality are real *relative* to different times. On this view, reality is composed of tensed facts, no time is privileged compared to others, and the world is a coherent one. It's just that whether some facts belong to reality is relative to what time it is. So my writing this book in the present is a fact, and it is one of the facts that makes up reality. But it is only one of the facts that makes up reality relative to a particular time. Relative to another time my writing the book is past, and the fact that it is past is a fact that contributes to making up reality.

Fragmentalism is the view that reality is irreducibly incoherent. We can get fragments of reality that are coherent, but there's no way of having all the facts that make up reality make sense together. This view embraces the contradiction that McTaggart was worried about. It is both the case that my writing the book is present and my writing the book is past. Reality includes both facts. We make sense of different times by considering different incompatible fragments of reality, but we can never coherently consider the whole of reality.

These two non-standard realisms about tense are supposed to provide a way where we can make sense of change over time, by having different facts being real at different times, or by having different fragments coherently describing different times. But on these views, it's still not clear why they count as a *dynamic* view. What feature of reality being relative to times, or fragmented into times, gives us a story about change in what time it is. Natalja Deng (2013a) argues that we should conclude that *no* description of reality can give the kind of dynamism that we ordinarily want. Fine's non-standard realisms give us 'a conceptual gesture' towards dynamism, and nothing more.

WHERE THIS LEAVES US

We've covered quite a lot of ground, so let's take a moment to recap, and think about where this leaves us. We have been discussing a debate about whether time does something –passing or flowing – that space doesn't do. One of the biggest challenges we've come across has been to state the disagreement.

- We have different views of what 'change' means.
- We have different overlapping distinctions between dynamic/static, A-theory/B-theory, and tensed/tenseless views.
- There's an argument that the passage of time is contradictory.
- There's an argument that time passing must have a rate at which it passes.
- There's an argument that if time passes, Presentism must be true.
- There's an argument that a complete description of reality, including a present time, isn't enough for time to pass.

It's easy to see why, in this debate, it is often not that there are two competing positions that we are weighing up evidence for, but a debate each side is confused by what the other means. Just getting the disagreement in focus is one of the major challenges!

A final worry looms. If framing the disagreements here is so hard, is that because there's simply no difference between the views in question? Craig Callender (2012) argues that there are three sorts of differences we should be looking for:

- Metaphysical differences
- Observational differences
- Explanatory differences

As we have seen, the metaphysics – the set of claims about the nature of the world – is very complicated. There's always the prospect that we will find a way to translate one view into another. Given that we're appealing to metaphors of flow and/or passage, working out what those metaphors stand for is difficult, and it's possible to use two different metaphors to describe exactly the same thing. Just because we use different language to describe two views is not enough to show they are not different descriptions of the same view. We need to show, in the way we characterise the views that they are really claiming something different about the world, rather than just using different language. Take the Growing-Block view and the Shrinking-Block view, for example. They appear to disagree strongly: one says the past exists and the future does not, and the other says that the future exists and the past does not. But what does 'exists' mean? If the two views mean something by existence, for example, they might not be disagreeing about metaphysics, just about the use of language.

If we can't frame the metaphysical differences, we should look for observational differences. But there don't seem to be many of these. In fact, both views set out to explain our observations of time, so they are alternative accounts of the same observations. There might be *future* observations that would make a difference. Even if two views are compatible with all the observations that we have so far, a difference in predictions would be useful. It might be that there are no differences in what they predict either. We should be a little cautious about predicting that there are no differences in prediction, however. Historically, humans have been bad at guessing what later humans will be able to predict with different resources of technology and ingenuity.

Our best hope, in the absence of observational differences, then, is to look for features of time that a dynamic view is able to explain better than a static view. Since dynamic views claim there is something – passage – that is not to be explained in terms of variation along a temporal dimension, the best way to make the case that these really are different views is by finding the places where 'passage' does explanatory work. In later chapters we will look at some of the cases where McTchange is supposed to offer explanatory differences.

QUESTIONS FOR DISCUSSION

1. What makes time different to space?
2. What role do metaphors play in accurately describing the world?
3. Do any of the arguments presented show that McTchange is incoherent?

NOTES

1 Broad (1959:766)
2 See Shardlow *et al.* (2021) for a study on ordinary people's views on the nature of time.
3 Callender (2017) frames things in this way, for example.
4 Gale (1968)
5 See e.g. Tim Maudlin (2002), Michael J. Raven (2011)
6 Defenders include Markosian (2004), Bourne (2006), Tallant (2014) and Ingram (2016, 2018).
7 Defenders include Broad (1923), Tooley (1998), Correia and Rosenkranz (2018) Forbes (2016).
8 Defenders include Cameron (2015) Miller (2019).
9 Defended by McCall (1994).
10 Defended by Casati and Torrengo (2011), Norton (2015), and Lam (2021).
11 Actually, I think the time I am editing it is present.
12 Correia and Rosenkranz (2013)
13 Hare (2018) argues that 'I' is not straightforward either.
14 This is in fact my response. See my (2016) and my (2023a).

FURTHER READING

Deng (2013a) discusses Fine's version of McTaggart's argument and questions what's at stake in the debate about whether time passes.

Olson (2009) gives an overview of the problems of the passage of time, including the problems of a rate of time's passage.

Sanford (1968) argues that McTaggart's argument is based on a confusion.

ATOMS AND CONTINUITY

Whether or not we think time *flows*, we might be interested in other properties of time. Terry Pratchett, in a footnote to one of his novels, jokes that 'The shortest unit of time in the multiverse is the New York Second, defined as the period of time between the traffic lights turning green and the cab behind you honking.'[1] But *is* there a shortest unit of time? Or given any unit of time, can we divide it into shorter units still? Are there indivisible units of time – time *atoms* – or is time infinitely divisible?[2] In this chapter we will be considering some of the puzzles associated with picking either option.

These puzzles, as we shall see, go back to some of the earliest Greek philosophers. Occasionally one finds claims to the effect that these puzzles have now been solved by the developments of modern mathematics.[3] It is likely that the initial statements of the problem involve some mathematical confusion. But I don't think the problems go away. And I don't think mathematics can settle for us whether or not we think time has a shortest unit, or is infinitely divisible. All it can do is give us tools to describe both options; the decision of which to accept is not a *mathematical* question.

DISCRETE, CONTINUOUS OR DENSE?

Let's get some mathematical distinctions out of the way, so they don't confuse us.

Time is **discrete** if and only if there is some time t_1 and some other time t_2 such that there are no times between t_1 and t_2.

DOI: 10.4324/9781003189459-2

Time is **dense** if and only if for all distinct times t_1 and t_2, there are
   countably many times between them.
Time is **continuous** if and only if for all distinct times t_1 and t_2
   there are uncountably many times between them.

The difference between time being discrete and the other two is
whether time is *infinitely divisible*. If time is discrete there is a smallest division of time – a time atom. If there are no time atoms, there
isn't a smallest unit of time, and time isn't discrete. The difference
between time being dense and time being continuous comes down
to a question about what kind of infinity we are interested in.

We can think about infinities using number series. Let's start with
the *natural numbers*; the number series that starts with 1 and adds 1
each time. So 1, 2, 3, 4, 5, 6, 7… etc. This sequence is infinitely long.
In fact, it's *countable* infinity. Although it would be impossible to ever
reach the end of the sequence, at any point in the sequence we get to
the next one by adding 1. Although the sequence is infinitely long, it
is discrete. The sequence of natural numbers has no numbers between
1 and 2. After 1, the very next number is 2. If time forms a sequence
like the natural numbers, time is discrete.

Let's think now of the rational numbers. That's the sequence of
numbers that includes all the natural numbers, 0 and the negative
equivalents of the natural numbers (-1, -2, -3, etc.), as well as all the
fractions ($\frac{1}{2}, \frac{1}{3}, \frac{1}{4}, \frac{2}{3}, \frac{3}{4}$ etc.). This sequence is also countably infinitely
long (because we can pair each number with one of the natural
numbers, and never run out of either). But unlike the natural numbers, there are a countably infinite number of numbers *between* any
two numbers. If time forms a sequence like the rational numbers,
time is dense.

Let's think about a final sequence of numbers, the real numbers.
This sequence has all the rational numbers, plus all the numbers
between them that can't be expressed as fractions (such as π or $\sqrt{2}$).
The real numbers are uncountably infinite; even if we paired each
one with a natural number, we would have an infinite number of
real numbers left.[4] If time forms a sequence like the real numbers,
time is continuous. A real-number-like sequence is called a continuum (plural: continua).

The Ancient Greeks were only considering whether time is discrete or dense. It's useful to be aware that time could also be

continuous. The mathematics for dealing with uncountable infinities is one of the areas that we have resources not open to the Ancient Greeks. It's not clear whether considering time as continuous makes the problems easier or harder, however.

As we'll see, the problems come arranged in two phalanxes.[5] If you accept that time is infinitely divisible, you must face one phalanx of problems. If you deny that time is infinitely divisible, you are forced to deal with the other phalanx. So whichever option you select, you are forced to defend yourself against these problems.

ZENO'S PARADOXES: TIME IS INFINITELY DIVISIBLE

Zeno of Elea lived in the 5th century BC in Elea, which is now part of southern Italy. We have very little of his own writing left, but he has become legendary as a philosopher due to his arguments for the impossibility of motion. I should warn you, before we continue, that many students get frustrated by these arguments (though perhaps you will be inured to this by the previous chapter). Obviously, in reading this very sentence, your eyes have moved across the page! Virtually none of the people discussing these arguments since Zeno agree with the conclusion that motion is impossible. It's easy to take these problems as riddles designed to annoy people (indeed that seems to have been how they were often regarded by Zeno's contemporaries). But these problems reward some patience.

THE DICHOTOMY

The dichotomy is one of the most famous of Zeno's paradoxes. It comes in two versions. The first version tries to show the impossibility of you moving some distance. Let's start with 100m, just because it's a nice round number. If time and space are infinitely divisible, in order to run 100m, you must first get halfway (50m). Then, you need to complete half the remaining journey (75m). After that you need to complete half of the remaining journey (87.5m), and then half the remainder again (93.75m), and half the remainder again (96.875m). Nearly there, you might think. But no. There are still an infinite number of points you have to pass to get

Figure 2.1 The dichotomy (1st version)

to 100m. And, Zeno argues, that you cannot pass an infinite number of points. So you cannot run 100m. (See Figure 2.1.)

The second version makes things even worse. Not only can you not *complete* your 100m run, but you cannot even *begin* it! In order to get halfway (50m) you have to have already got halfway there (25m). But in order to do that, you need to get halfway to there (12.5m), and in order to get even that far, you must get halfway (6.25m). To get that far you need to get halfway first (3.125m). And even to get that far you have to have completed an infinite number of smaller runs. Not only can you not complete any distance, but you can't even *start* running without doing the impossible. (See Figure 2.2.)

Aristotle's solution is to make a distinction between actual and potential tasks.[6] Although you *could* divide the 100m distance infinitely, running 100m doesn't involve running an infinite number of separate runs. It *would* be impossible if it did, but it doesn't, so that's fine.

Zeno's dichotomy rests on whether or not motion involves a *supertask*, i.e. a task that involves doing an infinite number of tasks in sequence. We have a limited number of options to respond:

- we deny that running 100m involves a supertask
- we deny that supertasks are impossible.
- we reject the claim that space is infinitely divisible
- we accept motion is impossible

Readers who have been paying attention will notice that the dichotomy is set up as an argument that takes *space* to be infinitely divisible.

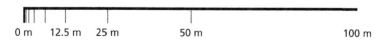

Figure 2.2 The dichotomy (2nd version)

But it is easy to do a version for time.[7] It doesn't even involve *attempting* to run. Waiting 2 minutes means passing through each moment for the first minute, which involves passing through each moment for the first 30s, which involves passing through each moment for the first 15s which involves passing through each moment for the first 7.5s. And there are still an infinite number of moments to get through in the first 7.5s! Not only can you not run 100m, but you can't wait for 2 minutes to pass, since even that is a supertask.

An important mathematical point to note here: we don't establish the duration of a continuous period of time by *adding up* all the moments; we *measure* durations rather than add them up. The error with Zeno's dichotomy is to think that for motion to take place, or for time to pass, we must add up all the points (and so complete a supertask), but measuring a duration doesn't require adding up each point, and so doesn't involve a supertask.

THE ACHILLES

Zeno's second argument claims it is impossible too for the fastest runner (Achilles in ancient Greece, Bolt at time of writing) to catch the slowest runner (a tortoise) if the tortoise has a head start. If we assume that Achilles is running at a constant speed, and starts 10m behind the tortoise, he will catch up to where the tortoise was after a certain amount of time. But by that point the tortoise will have moved, and Achilles will have to get to that point. And by the time he has done that, the tortoise will also have moved. Once again, it looks like motion involves a supertask.

The options are the same here as for the dichotomy. One response you might have, to both of these arguments, is that it is only impossible to complete these supertasks if one has a finite series of moments in which to do it. But if one has an infinite number of tasks and an infinite number of moments, completing a supertask should be fine, you might think.

THOMSON'S LAMP

It is not the case that completing a supertask requires an infinite amount of time. As we saw above, waiting for two minutes is a candidate supertask. If time is infinitely divisible, you might think it is possible to complete a supertask in two minutes. But this would be a mistake. It's not impossible to complete a supertask because it is too long, but because it is *incompletable*. Thomson's lamp illustrates this.

James Thomson (1954) asks us to imagine a lamp with a single button, the pressing of which turns the light on if it is off, and off if it is on. We start by turning the lamp on, waiting for a minute, and turning the lamp off, waiting 30s, turning it on, waiting 15s, turning it off, waiting 7.5s, turning in on, etc. Each time, we press the button after half the interval we waited previously. The whole sequence will last 2 minutes. 1 minute + 30s + 15s + 7.5s + 3.75s… is an infinite sequence that converges on a finite limit: 2 minutes. The problem with completing such a supertask is not that it takes infinitely long. The problem is that it is impossible to complete. This becomes clear when we ask a very simple question. At the end of 2 minutes, is the lamp on or off?

If the lamp is on, the sequence is unfinished, because it should have been followed by the lamp turning off. If the lamp is off, the sequence is unfinished, because it should have been finished by the lamp turning on. Because it is an infinite sequence, there is no *last* moment in the sequence. That's why it cannot be completed. If Thompson's argument is right, the response to the dichotomy and the Achilles is to reject the claim that both involve actual supertasks, but only potentially infinitely many tasks. Alternatively, we can reject the claim that time is infinitely divisible.

ZENO'S PARADOXES: TIME HAS A SMALLEST DURATION

Let's confront the other phalanx of arguments. What if time has a shortest duration? We no longer have to worry about the impossibility of supertasks. Instead, different problems arise for time.

THE ARROW

Imagine a snapshot of an arrow flying through the air. This snapshot is of the arrow for one time atom – the shortest possible duration. The problem is traditionally framed in what might seem an

Figure 2.3 The arrow

odd way. The arrow in the snapshot takes up a space *equal to itself*. I had a dog once that despite being quite a small dog could take up an entire sofa. Wherever you would try and sit, it would turn out the dog was there. The dog could achieve this by moving around the sofa. But the arrow in our snapshot can't take up a space greater than itself, because in order to do that it would have to move around the space. Some time would need to pass in order for it to move. We are dealing with one time atom, so there are no sub-units of time in which the arrow can be in different places. (See Figure 2.3.)

Given any such snapshot, the arrow isn't moving *during* that snapshot. Perhaps the arrow moves *in between* the snapshots? Given we are dealing with discrete time, we can compare two time atoms that are next to each other, and there simply is no 'in between' during which the arrow can fly. If it can't fly during the snapshots, and it can't fly between the snapshots, the argument goes, it can't fly. So the flying arrow can never fly.

One response here is to pay very close attention to the language that we use. It might be true that an arrow cannot fly *during* a snapshot, but it might be true of the arrow that it is flying *at* the time of the snapshot. That is, we can think that the snapshot in Figure 2.3 needs a little note adding, telling us what the velocity of the arrow is.

Lots of people think that response is the right one, but I'm not so sure. Being in motion is not a property of some state of the arrow; the very idea of a 'state of motion' is confused. Suppose motion is just a matter of being in different places at different times. That we have a sequence of snapshots, each with the arrow being in a different location, is all that we need for motion, according to this response.[8]

This is the second of the places where the 'modern mathematics saves the day' story comes in. Previously we saw that measure theory means we don't have to add up the points in a continuum. Here the idea of instantaneous velocity is the key one. From Aristotle until Newton, the idea of an instantaneous velocity was considered conceptually problematic.[9] Following the development of calculus, we can assign a velocity to something at a moment by using differentiation: $\frac{dy}{dx}$. We can treat the time atom as the limit duration of a longer change in time, and the position of the arrow as a limit of a variation in location over different snapshots. So, we can give a mathematical value to the arrow at a snapshot, without thinking that it needs to involve a *state* of motion.

It's not clear that we have escaped our problems yet, however. The velocity of the arrow at our snapshot is *derivative* of its position at other snapshots. So what the arrow is doing now depends on other times. The concept of a *phase-space*, often used in physics, gives the location and position of all the entities in a system at a particular snapshot of time, and, with the laws that operate in that system, allows us to derive the positions and velocities of all the entities at all other times. Mathematically, this is unproblematic. But if the phase-space is derivative of the other times, we can't also derive other times from the phase-space. If the lesson of Zeno's arrow is taken to be that velocity at a time depends on where something is at other times, what happens at those other times cannot also depend on the velocity of that thing at the time under consideration. The problem isn't with thinking that the arrow has a velocity at a time, but that it can have a velocity at a time that is not derived from some change over time.

THE STADIUM

Imagine you have gone to observe a demonstration of close-formation marching. You see three lines of tightly packed soldiers. One line (the As) standing still, and two other lines (the Bs and Cs) coming from the sides to take up position directly behind the As. The manoeuvre is nearly complete. Soldier A_2 has soldier B_3 directly behind them, and soldier C_1 is directly behind soldier B_3. All that remains for the manoeuvre is for C_1 to lead the C row in moving one place to the left, and for B_3 and the B row to move one place to the right, so that B_1 and C_1 are lined up behind A_1, and B_3 and C_3 are lined up behind A_3. But when I say that they are tightly packed, I really mean it. In fact, we are to imagine that each soldier takes up precisely one space atom; there is no gap in between

Figure 2.4 The stadium

the soldiers. When a soldier moves from one place to another, they are moving to the next place, and there is no intermediate place between them, through which they pass. (See Figure 2.4.)

What's the paradox? Well, when C_1 moves one place to the left, and B_3 to move one place to the right, C_1 passes B_2, and B_3 passes C_2. But C_1 is never next to B_2, and B_3 is never next to C_2. They pass each other without ever being opposite each other. That's not how we normally think passing works!

This is a paradox about motion in atomic space, but we can come up with a version that more obviously involves time. We can say that some event is in the past without ever being present, for example. If an event is complete when all its phases exist (for example on the Growing-Block view discussed in ch.1), sufficiently short events that have a single phase one time–atom long become past without ever being present. There is never a time when some of the event exists, but not all phases do (which is what would be required for the event being present) so the event goes from being future (no phases existing, the event yet to happen) to past (all phases existing, the event having happened) without any intermediate period when the event is present (some, but not all phases existing, the event currently happening). Things shouldn't become past, without first being present, but if we think of events that have the smallest possible duration, it seems they do.

WEYL TILES

A more contemporary argument with a Greek flavour comes from Herman Weyl. Weyl presents an argument that space can't be discrete, by asking us to imagine doing geometry in a space made up of atomic discrete tiles.[10] The argument requires a well-known piece of mathematics: Pythagoras' theorem: $a^2 + b^2 = c^2$. (The maths, at least, does come from ancient Greece!) Consider how we make triangles in space: We make a right-angled triangle one space-atom tall, and one space-atom wide. By Pythagoras' theorem, we can calculate the length of the hypotenuse: $1 + 1 = 2 = c^2$. But the length of the hypotenuse for a 1x1 right-angled triangle, Pythagoras' theorem tells us, is $\sqrt{2}$. And when we were explaining what it was for a space to be discrete, this was one of the examples of a length that discrete space couldn't have. You can't have discrete right-angled triangles that obey Pythagoras's theorem!

You might hope that this problem is just because we are dealing with very small scales. But geometry throws up such problems for even very large discrete shapes. Weyl tiles are sometimes jocularly called 'Wail tiles', because of the frustration they cause those attempting geometry in discrete space!

THE MILLSTONE

The problem of irrational numbers needed to make sense of geometry is anticipated much earlier, during the Golden Age of Baghdad, in the 9th century. Ibrahim Al-Nazzam argues against an atomistic view by considering a millstone.[11] This large, and very solid, bit of rock rotates, such that a point on the outside of the rock moves faster than a point near the middle. If the point on the outside is occupying one atom of space per one atom of time, the points inside must be moving slower than that. This means that they must be moving discontinuously, lingering at the same space atom for multiple time atoms, and then leaping to the next one. Alternatively, if the point near the middle is moving at one space atom per time atom, the outside of the millstone must leap over space atoms without passing through them. Either way, the apparently solid millstone's parts stop being next to each other each time it rotates. The only way for the atomist about space and time to allow for the millstone to rotate is by breaking it into fragments that move at different speeds.

Like the hypotenuse of a triangle, the geometry of a circle requires the use of irrational numbers. In this case, the ratio between the circumference and the diameter: π. Any atomist about space and time needs to deal with the fact that our geometry presupposes continuous spaces and times.

QUANTUM GRAVITY

The thought might have occurred to you that speculating about whether matter is infinitely divisible is unhelpful. We should observe the world, and study how it works. It is not quite so simple as that, both because when studying the world we bring many pre-suppositions with us, and also when we study the world what we find is stranger than we might have expected. In this section, we will briefly sketch some of the challenges for thinking about the paradoxes we have encountered once we look at our best physical theories of space and time.

We need to start with a few key ideas from contemporary physics, expressed with the minimum of technicality.

The **General Theory of Relativity** is a physical account of how space and time relate to gravity. Space and time can't be separated from each other (we call the combination 'space–time') on this theory, nor from gravity, which deforms space–time. Massive objects (i.e. objects with mass) curve space–time around them in a way that is described by the General Theory of Relativity. The key thought here (to which we will return in ch. 5) is that we can't describe space, time, and matter separately.

Quantum Theory is our best theory of the nature of matter in the Universe. It says that matter/energy are not infinitely divisible, but have smallest units. These are called 'quanta' because the Greek term we have been using for indivisible units – 'atoms' – was already taken by the particles made of protons, neutrons and elections, which turned out to be divisible after all.

Quantum theory says that mass/energy are discrete, but also describes a range of surprising phenomena. Two particularly interesting results will be useful now:

Heisenberg's Uncertainty Principle says that we can't precisely know both something's location and its momentum.[12] This is because attempting to measure one affects the other.

The **Planck-length** (1.616255×10^{-35} m) is the smallest measurable unit of distance (with **Planck-time** being the amount of time it takes light (the fastest thing there is) to travel 1 Planck-length in a vacuum).[13]

So, we have an account of how matter works according to which it is impossible to come up with very precise locations without large amounts of momentum, and there is a smallest measurable distance available to us. So far this is compatible with space–time being continuous. *Measuring* minute distances might be impossible but they may be, for mathematical purposes, infinitely divisible. In fact, in standard treatments of quantum theory, space–time is treated as a continuous structure.[14]

When we combine the General Theory of Relativity with Quantum Theory we get **Quantum Gravity**. In Quantum Gravity we treat space–time itself as being subject to quantum theory. This means that in Quantum Gravity space–time is treated as being quantised (i.e. as having space–time atoms). Because of Heisenberg's Uncertainty Principle, in order to get precision of the location of any particle with mass at below Planck-length/Planck-time scales we would need lots of momentum, which, according to the General Theory of Relativity, would distort the space–time. This means that when we attempt to measure any particle smaller than a Planck-length, it is effectively hidden within its own miniature black hole of distorted space–time. In fact, it turns out that there's no way to give physical meaning to distances shorter than a Planck-length or durations shorter than a Planck-time. At such scales, the concepts of distance or duration with which we set up Zeno's paradoxes cease to be meaningful. Space–time can't be infinitely divisible, because at a certain point, it ceases to *count* as space–time.

So, on Quantum Gravity we find that space–time is quantised, and 'fuzzy' (as a result of Heisenberg's Uncertainty Principle) at very small (i.e. close to Planck-length) scales.

As Carlo Rovelli and Francesca Vidotto put it (2015:8):

> We need a genuinely new way of doing physics, where space and time come *after*, and not *before*, the quantum states... The quantum states are not quantum states *on* spacetime. They are quantum states *of* spacetime.

Quantum Gravity has more troubles for us in store. Two more quantum effects deserve brief mention.

Non-locality is a phenomenon where there seems to be no precise location for certain events. In particular, two quantum 'particles' become *entangled* such that interacting with one affects the properties of the other. Once these 'particles' are entangled, they can be arbitrary distances from one another, while still mutually affecting one another. One possible response is to reject the talk of 'particles' (in favour of 'fields', perhaps), but in any case the idea that we are going to build up what is happening in normal (i.e. medium-sized) cases from what is happening at very, very precise locations doesn't fit with our understanding of quantum mechanics.[15]

The *time order* in which things happens also seems to be undermined by quantum theory. There are cases, like the *delayed double-slit experiment*, where it seems like we have a sequence of events, but we can't give them an ordering. Let's start with the standard double-slit experiment. (See Figure 2.5.)

In this experiment, light is shone at a screen. This screen has two very thin slits in it, which can be covered up. When either one is open, we can observe that light creates a diffraction pattern, spreading out from the slit, as we would expect when a wave passes through a gap of similar size to the wavelength. When both slits are open, we get an interference pattern, suggesting that there are two waves interacting with each other as a result of diffracting when coming out of the two slits. But when we restrict the amount of

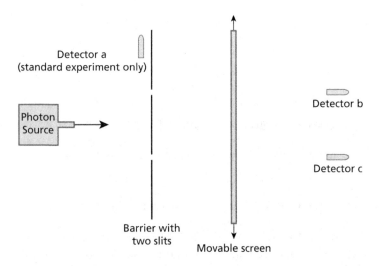

Figure 2.5 The delayed double-slit experiment

light to a single quantum of energy, we get a single dot of light on the other side. This suggests that we have a single particle. But as we repeat this a single quantum of light (i.e. a *photon*) at a time, *we still see these interference effects*. It is as if a single light particle has gone through both slits! This is often described as **wave–particle duality.** In practice, as with non-locality, the solution might be to think that the concepts of wave and particle, that were useful concepts in earlier physics at bigger scales, just aren't that helpful in thinking carefully about quantum scales.

One of the striking things about wave-particle duality is that when we try to take measurements of what's going on in the middle of the double-slit experiment (labelled 'detector a'), we affect things, such that the interference patterns stop happening. In the theoretical jargon, they talk about the '*wave-function collapsing*'. When we take measurements as things go through the slits, we get effects more like particles than like waves. One of the central philosophical problems for quantum mechanics is of how to think about what takes place when these wave-functions are not being measured.[16] Those issues won't be our concern here. But it's striking that there seems to be lots of flexibility around when we do the measuring.

John Wheeler (1978) proposed an experiment in which we set up the double slit apparatus without detector a, such that we can change whether there is a detection screen after the slits very easily. We then detect the photons some distance behind the screen (detectors b and c). The thought is that we seem to be able to affect whether the photon passing through the slit(s) appears wave-like or particle-like by what we do to the detection screen *after* the two slits. When we remove the screen, we no longer get evidence of the interference pattern in the detectors that were previously behind the screen. Huw Price (1996) argues that this is evidence of backwards causation, though this view is not widely accepted. It does create a challenge for thinking of this set up as involving a series of separate episodes, however. We might be tempted to say *first* the light goes through one slit (or two slits), and *then* it hits the detection screen and produces a pattern. But the delayed double-slit experiment shows the presence of the detection screen is not independent from the photon's path towards it. The ordering of them into a sequence might not make sense. Perhaps the 'sequence' of events in such experiments is not divisible into a series of sub-events after all.

The physical issues here get quite technical, and there are many competing interpretations available. But it is useful to see that many of the issues raised by the paradoxes and puzzles we have considered are still relevant to our best physics. In some sense, Quantum Gravity simply seems to accept lots of the conclusions of Zeno's paradoxes at face-value. In Quantum Gravity, there are no super-tasks, because there are no continua. It doesn't make sense to talk of movement at a snapshot of time, and it is the case that things get to pass each other without ever being next to each other.

TA NUN – 'THE NOW'

So far, we have been treating the question of whether space and time are infinitely divisible as if it were totally separate from the discussions of McTchange in the previous chapter. What if we think there is a unique present? Does it have earlier and later parts, or is it partless? Jonathan Lear (1981) pointed out a subtle question of translation that affects how we view Zeno's paradoxes. '*ta nun*', literally 'the now', had been translated as 'the instant' in standard discussions of Zeno's arrow. But if instead it was translated as 'the present moment', the paradox starts to look very different. As Robin Le Poidevin (2002) went on to argue, this affects what role the paradoxes play in the philosophy of time.

Whether or not we think this is how we *ought* to translate Zeno's paradoxes, in this section we'll consider what happens to them if we think of them as appealing to a dynamic view of time with a unique and objective present moment.

The problem of supertasks looks particularly pressing if each point in the continuum must be successively present (however briefly). The claim that the present has literally no duration allows for continuum-many instants to occur within a finite time. But if the present is somehow privileged, by being unlike other times, or being the only time that really exists, its having literally no dura-tion seems to be a problem. As we saw above, instants work best as limits of intervals, rather than trying to build up intervals out of instants.

But there seems to be something odd about calling an interval present. If it has earlier and later parts, it looks like some of those parts are not present; either they are past or future. As Augustine of

Hippo observed, a century being present has years that are past and/or years that are future. And those years have months that are past and/or months that are future, and those months have days that are past and/or days that are future, those days have hours that are past and/or hours that are future. For any interval we call 'the present' it seems to be decomposable into sub-intervals that are not present because they are past, and sub-intervals not present because they are future.[17] The present disappears.

You might think the present has a duration and it is the duration of conscious awareness. The problems with this is that the duration of conscious awareness – known as the *specious present* – varies greatly. Different people in the same room can be experiencing it very differently, and the same person can experience it differently depending on their mood and what they are paying attention to. If we tie the present to the specious present, we make what is present different for different people.

If the arrow in Zeno's arrow only flies when it is present, and the present is partless (the arrow takes up a space equal to itself) we end up with a situation where it appears that the arrow isn't flying because of its present properties, but because of properties it used to have or will have. The present, the time that should be easiest for us to grasp, turns out to depend on what has happened or what will happen.

One radical solution is to get rid of the idea of the present time all together. Rather than thinking that there are some times that have this property of being present or not being present, we might think that presentness is a property of things happening, as Nicky Kroll (2020) suggests. Rather than trying to build up happenings out of partless presents, we build up presents out of happenings.

I think this view helps us move away from the problems of trying to answer how long the present is. But it does seem to have the consequence that some events come to have happened without ever being present.

CONCLUDING REMARKS

We started with a question: 'Does time have a smallest unit?'. This question took us on a journey through Ancient Greek philosophy through to contemporary physics. It was probably a frustrating journey; both the Ancient Greek philosophy and the quantum physics are challenging simply to wrap one's head around. But there are some lessons we can take away:

- If space–time is infinitely divisible, we have to respond to the worry that supertasks are impossible.
- If space–time is not infinitely divisible, we need to respond to worries about irrational values that are used in geometry.
- If we think there is an objective present time, we need to say how long it is.
- If our best physics says that distance and duration don't make sense at very small scales, we need to make sense of how they emerge at bigger scales.

As with many philosophical questions, while it's possible to introduce the puzzles without much technical detail, coming up with satisfactory answers may require conceptual resources we have not developed yet.

QUESTIONS FOR DISCUSSION

1. What is an atom of time?
2. Can we dismiss Zeno's arguments by demonstrating that motion is possible?
3. Does an arrow fly at an instant?
4. Can things become past without first being present?
5. Can physical experiments tell us that time is continuous or that it is discrete?

NOTES

1 Pratchett (1992: 290)
2 'Atom' here is used in the original Greek sense of something that is indivisible. Not to be confused with the particle made up of protons, neutrons, and electrons.
3 E.g. Peirce (1935, vol VI §177, p.122); Grünbaum (1968); Falletta (1983: 189).
4 In mathematical terms, there is no bijection from the real numbers to the natural numbers, Cantor's diagonalisation proof is a surprisingly intuitive argument for this. See Cantor (1891).
5 It is disputed, e.g. by Sorabji (1983:331), that this is how we should interpret Zeno's treatment of the paradoxes. I present them in this way, because I think it is the most compelling way to treat them, rather than because I think it the most historically accurate.

6 Cf. Sorabji (1983:322)
7 Cf. Sorabji (1983:322)
8 Cf. Russell (1903:473)
9 Owen (1958: 221)
10 Salmon (1980) has a clean statement of the Weyl Tile argument. See also McDaniel (2007).
11 Sorabji (1983: ch.25)
12 Momentum = (mass × velocity)
13 Pratchett was wrong; the New York second is not the smallest time-interval.
14 Albert (1992:46 fn.9)
15 Albert (1992 ch.3)
16 Albert (1992) is an excellent introduction to these issues.
17 *Confessions*: 11.15.19–20

FURTHER READING

Sainsbury (2009) contains a chapter on Zeno's paradoxes that is a good place to start.

For a more thoroughly mathematical treatment Grünbaum (1986) is a classic text.

For classical scholarship on these problems Sorabji (1983) is excellent.

EXPERIENCING CHANGE

Why should we believe time passes in the sense discussed in chapter 1? Why should we believe that there is McTchange – the change characteristic of time passing? A natural thought is that it is something about our experience that suggests time passes. Indeed, people have often thought that we might believe that there is McTchange because we have evidence from perception that there is McTchange. After all, we see things change all the time!

In this chapter, we will consider our perceptual experience of change, and consider some problems with thinking it is evidence for there being McTchange. But before that let's consider some important distinctions.

Perceptual experiences, as contrasted with, for example, memory and anticipation, are experiences that present the world as being a certain way. Memories (at least *episodic memories* – memories of particular episodes) present the world as having been a certain way. Anticipations predict that the world will be a certain way.

In the case of episodic memories and perceptual experiences, there's a thought that if they are genuine memories or genuine perceptual experiences, they are *factive*. That is, genuine perceptions and genuine memories truly present the world as being/having been a certain way. This is sometimes at odds with how we talk. A politician might apologise for 'the perception of inappropriate behaviour' despite claiming that there has been no inappropriate behaviour. Here they are contrasting what really happened with how it appeared. As we shall be using the term, if you 'perceive' something, then that wasn't a mere appearance. On this factive reading of perception, we might not know what it is we perceive,

DOI: 10.4324/9781003189459-3

since we may be misled by mere appearances. If you genuinely perceive something, things are as you perceive them to be.[1] So too with memories; we can *confabulate* something. That is, we can think we remember, but actually it just *seems* to us like we remember. If you genuinely remember, the thing you remember happened. Anticipations, by contrast, are not factive. If you genuinely anticipate something happening that does not mean that it will happen.

There's a view of perception and memory where what we do is suck vast amounts of information about the world in, and then form a model or *representation* of the world that either *corresponds* to the world or fails to correspond.[2] This is almost certainly not how perception or memory work.[3] Memory and perception rely much more on anticipation than such a picture would suggest. They also rely on knowledge of how to get around and manipulate the world, not merely on mental depictions or descriptions of it. Nonetheless, memory and perception both involve someone relating to the world in a successful way. Memory and perception both involve getting something right about the world. The term '*veridical*' is used for the way in which they get things right. Perception and memory are factive because they have to be veridical to count as perceptions/memories. Anticipation merely attempts to get something right, but anticipating something that never happens is still a genuine anticipation.

Perception is one specific type of experience, but we might think that we have experiences of time in a much broader sense. We might find that our lives fall into certain rhythms, and our behaviour is governed by different time-constraints. We might find that, at different stages of our life-course, we are disposed to feel very differently about our lives. All of this would rightly be included under the heading 'temporal experience'. But in this chapter, it is perception in particular that we will focus on.

Why focus so heavily on perception? All the various phenomena that count as temporal experience give us reason to think that time is interesting, and that it differs in some ways (at least for creatures like us) from space. But perception is meant to provide evidence that there is McTchange in a way that that other bits of temporal experience do not. It is a historical fluke of Western culture that we have weekends on Saturdays and Sundays, and a 'working week' from Monday to Friday, with a distinction between office hours and leisure time. These features of our culture are interesting, and they clearly have effects on how our societies are organised and how our lives go. But things could have developed differently. When we investigate these phenomena, we find out interesting things about our culture. But if we want to find something out about the nature of time, regardless of culture, focussing on the perceptual evidence we have about time seems a more straightforward place to begin.[4]

Do we have perceptual evidence for McTchange? I'm going to suggest that we don't. But I don't think that is a reason *not* to believe in McTchange. It's just that we won't find reasons to believe in McTchange just by having them pop up in our visual field, as if they had been hiding behind a bush.

WHAT SORTS OF TEMPORAL FEATURES DO WE PERCEIVE?

Having narrowed ourselves down to perceptual experience of time, it's worth noting how many different phenomena we're still left with.

Qualitative change is change in the qualities of an object. So when we experience a tone change pitch, or leaves change colour, we are experiencing a change in qualities.

Movement is a change in location of an object (or change in location of parts of an object).

In these cases, we can have an experience of something moving, or changing qualities, or merely an experience of having moved or having changed. When we look at an analogue clock, for example, we might see the second hand has moved, but not see the hour hand move. Nonetheless, we might notice that the hour hand is in a different position to what it was when we previously looked.

Lasting describes something not changing for a period of time.

It might seem odd to have this as a perceptual experience, but just as we can notice that something has changed, we can notice that it hasn't changed.

Coming to be describes the change of a new object forming.

Ceasing to be describes the change of an object being destroyed.

It's not just the qualities and locations of things changing that we can perceive, but also the number of things.

In addition to awareness of change in different ways, we can be aware of other temporal features of experience.

Temporal Order is whether events come before or after other events. So we can notice that events come in a sequence, for example, or that they are out of sequence.

Succession is very similar to order, but importantly distinct. Succession is something happening and then something else happening.

Succession presupposes order, but lots of things come in orders. The tallest buildings in the world have an ordering from tallest to 2nd tallest to 3rd tallest, etc. But that's not the same as saying first one was tallest, *then* another was tallest, and *then* the next was. Succession involves not just order but happening followed by happening.

Presence is just the minimal experience of something being presented in experience.

Note that when we look at the stars, the light from the starts has travelled for years, perhaps thousands of years, to reach your eyes. The stars seem to be present in experience, even though we might want to claim that the events we are seeing are now past.

Flow is an experience of time passing.

Flow, as a feature of experience, is an awareness of urgency, rather than straightforwardly a perception of McTchange. So, when you are nervous time seems to busy and lots is happening, time seems to whizz by, and when you are bored, time seems to crawl.

So far, we have been considering the *contents* of experience; that which is presented in experience. But time might show up in the *way* things are presented in experience. Giuliano Torrengo (2017) argues that we can think of flow not as something presented in experience, but as a 'phenomenal modifier', a way our experience is presented. Just as when our vision is blurry we don't think that the things presented to us are blurry, we shouldn't think flow is something in experience that we are aware of, but a modification of the way we experience whatever it is we experience.

Which of those features gives us the best evidence for McTchange? Succession seems to be the closest to McTchange. If we (genuinely) perceive succession in experience, *and* we can't explain succession in terms of mere temporal variation, then experience gives us evidence of McTchange.

TEMPORAL MISPERCEPTIONS

If we perceive succession, and we can't explain succession without appealing to McTchange, then we have reason to believe in McTchange. As we discussed above, perception is factive. It could be that we have experiences which *seem* to be perceptual, but in fact aren't. Let's briefly run through different ways in which we can misperceive things in this section.

> **Illusions** are cases when there is something that you perceive, but it appears in a way that is misleading.

Consider optical illusions, such as the 'rotating snakes illusion', where we look at a static image, (in this case one that depicts a series of coiled snakes), but it appears to contain movement. (See Figure 3.1)[5]

In that case, we are really perceiving a picture, but it appears to move when it does not. In fact, the apparent movement is an effect of our eyes moving.

Another illusion, the '*phi* phenomenon', involves two distinct flashes of light. There is a first flash followed by a second flash off to one side. If the circumstances are right, it appears as though a dot is moving from the position of the first flash to the position of the second. In this case we are really perceiving light, but it appears as if there is one persisting, moving, light-source, rather than two distinct unmoving light sources. There are many other similar illusions, where we experience movement when nothing is in fact moving. Appeals to our experience of change can be dismissed as mere illusions of change if we can explain them as arising from unchanging phenomena.

> **Hallucinations** are cases where it appears that there is something, when really there is nothing beyond the appearance.

Figure 3.1 The rotating snakes illusion

Sean Power (2018: 173) argues there are no temporal hallucinations. The thought here is that temporal hallucinations would involve hallucinating an object which was time, but time is the wrong kind of thing, he claims, to be an object of experience. Nonetheless, we might hallucinate objects other than time which have relevant temporal properties. If we hallucinate a shimmering oasis, the shimmering is a qualitative change. If we hallucinate pink elephants dancing, the dancing is a movement. If the evidence for McTchange stems from our experience of things changing, it could be that we merely hallucinate such changes.

Anosognosia refers to cases where something that is presented in experience does not get recognised.

One of the most striking instances of temporal anosognosia is motion blindness. Oliver Sacks (1970) reported having a migraine during which he saw moving objects as 'a series of stills'. Obviously, to those who can't experience movement in this way, driving and crossing the road are more dangerous than they otherwise would have been. A car coming towards them, for example, progressively takes up more of their visual field, but it is as if there is a succession of snapshots, rather than a persisting car changing location.

As Power (2018) points out, temporal anosognosia and temporal illusions are related. If there is an illusion that something still is moving, there may also be anosognosia that something moving is stationary. This is because the relevant temporal properties often have opposites which are also temporal properties.[6]

These three categories: illusion, hallucination and anosognosia, give someone denying the existence of McTchange the resources to block a move from an appearance of McTchange to the reality of McTchange. Let's now look at the most crucial phenomenon that is difficult to explain in terms of mere temporal variation: succession.

EXPERIENCE OF SUCCESSION

William James (1890:629) quotably observed that 'experience of succession is not a succession of experience'. Experiencing things *as if* they follow one after another is not the same as experiencing one thing, and then, after that, experiencing another. There could be a single moment that seems as if it was *just after* something, and *just before* something else, but without any actual change. Equally, there could be a series of moments, one after another, that we experience in turn without us being aware at any other time of other moments in the sequence. Our experience of succession, leaving the issue of McTchange aside for a while, needs explaining.

Think about listening to a tune. You seem to be aware in experience not just of a single note, but of that note following on from a previous one, and on the cusp of being followed by another one. It's not simply that, *in addition* to what's presented in experience, you have a memory of previous notes, and an anticipation of others, but that the way the note you are listening to *currently sounds* is affected by the notes you have just heard and the notes you anticipate. You hear the note as belonging to a sequence, and as part of an experience of succession.

How does this work? There are two main accounts of how we experience succession. One is an *extensional account*, in which we experience an extended period of time including the present along with a bit of the recent past and a bit of the immediate future. This is inspired by the writing of William James, and is also known as a 'specious present' account. The other is a *retentional* account, also known as a memory account.[7] This account, on which we don't experience an extended present, but instead experience the present as containing 'retentions' of the past, and 'protensions' (anticipations) of the future. This is inspired by the writing of Edmund Husserl.

EXTENSIONAL ACCOUNTS

The extensionalist claims we experience some duration in perception *as a whole*. There is some temporally extended period of time which we are aware of *as a unified experience*. If we take the sequence of notes in our melody, the idea is that we can be aware of multiple notes in experience, as unified, but still in sequence (i.e. not a chord). So, despite the fact the notes take place at different times, a single experience includes them all. This means the experienced present ('the specious present') has some duration. This duration is almost certainly different from duration the objective present has (if there is one).[8]

On this view it is like there is a moving window that includes some of the recent past and some anticipations of the future. For any time, at that time we will be aware of that time, what has just happened, and anticipate what's about to happen, in a single unified experience.

RETENTIONALIST ACCOUNTS

Retentional accounts, unlike extensional ones, don't require us to be aware of an *extended* period of time. On this view, present experience includes components that are *directed towards* the past and future.

The idea that thoughts can be 'directed' might seem strange. One way of thinking about it is that your thoughts are about something besides themselves; they 'point beyond' themselves. But part of what we should have in mind here is not just the images or words in someone's head, but the way they are primed for action in the world. Directedness towards the world, in the sense Husserl was interested in, involves approaching, expecting, and responding to the world in certain ways. So, for example, if you see an object that looks three-dimensional, you expect it to have sides that you can't currently see. And that expectation is part of your current experience, the object *looks as if* you could go round the back. Similarly, if you see a magician's top hat, it looks as if it couldn't contain a rabbit without you noticing. These appearances might not be perceptual experiences; the magician's hat merely appears empty. But these experiences shape how you interact with the things you see.

The retentionalist claims that present experiences have 'retentions' of the past (i.e. directedness towards the immediate past) and 'protentions' of the immediate future (i.e. anticipations of what is just about to happen). So each moment of experience is a stack of perceptual awareness of what is going on now, retentions of what just happened, and protentions of what is about to happen (along with all the other non-perceptual things built into experiences; moods, evaluations, pre-occupations, etc.).

These retentions are similar to perceptual states, in that they are meant to give us evidence of what the immediate past was like, just as perceptual states give us evidence of what is happening now. But perceptual states seem to be present in experience, whereas we are aware of retentions as presenting something *earlier* than what's presented to us in perception.

THE ROLE OF CHANGE ON BOTH HUSSERL'S AND JAMES'S VIEWS

The debate in the philosophy of perception about our experience of succession is often separate from debates about the nature of change. It can be presented with an assumption about whether McTchange exists, or as neutral with respect to that debate. Sometimes it is presented as affecting the debate over which times exist. Extensional views seem to commit one to multiple times existing and retentional views don't.[9]

James and Husserl, who originated these views, would probably have both been defenders of McTchange.[10] James (1909:213), for example, says: 'I myself find no good warrant for even suspecting the existence of any reality of a higher denomination than that distributed and strung-along and flowing sort of reality which we finite beings swim in.'

CONTEMPORARY DEFENCES

The debate continues as a live discussion amongst philosophers and psychologists today.[11] Le Poidevin (2007), Hoerl (2013), Phillips (2014), Dainton (2022), Power (2018) all defend views that are broadly extentional (in that they think we need durations of time to experience a sequence of musical notes as a single experience). Le Poidevin is clear that he thinks that although we are aware of some duration of time, the sense that there is some additional feeling of succession is a projection onto the world. Power (2015) argues that our ability to see standing waves (where something, is moving in a fixed pattern so quickly it appears to create an unmoving shape) suggests that we must experience multiple times in a single unified experience. In both cases, they think that we can explain our experience without appeal to McTchange. Ian Phillips (2014) rejects the claim that we need to have an awareness of unity *at* a time. Experiences are things that go on through time, on his view. Once we reject the claim that we have a succession of distinct experiences *at* a succession of times, the challenge of explaining how we can have an experience of succession goes. We just have a succession of experiences.

There's a group of cognitive scientists who offer defences of retentionalist models, based much more on treating the brain as a dynamical system than on paying careful attention to our experience.[12] On this approach, the question is not so much how to explain our experience of the unity of successive notes in a melody, but to explain, computationally, how a brain can retain information from states that it has updated from. The connection between these computational systems and perceptual experience would need some considerable spelling out, and so might not be in competition with the various accounts on offer.

Indeed, it's unclear whether we should expect our account of the cognitive mechanisms involved in our experience of change to commit us either way to whether change is understood as McTchange or mere temporal variation. Hoerl (2013) argues that the debate in fact lines up with disagreements about how to understand the nature of perception. Those who think of perception as relating us to the world in the right kind of way are more likely, Hoerl claims, to be extentionalists, whereas those who think that perception is about the brain representing the world are more likely to be retentionalists. When I framed things earlier, it was with perception being a way we relate to the world, though I didn't say anything that ruled out representations being involved in the mechanisms by which we relate to the world. Hoerl may be right about how these contemporary debates line up. Husserl is an odd choice as a figure head for the view that perception is all about representations in the brain, however he is one of the fiercest critics of that view! Contemporary writers defending views more directly inspired by Husserl than by cognitive science, such as McInerney (1991) and Zahavi (2007), are likely to think of perception as a way of relating to things in the world, rather than as representing it.

PROSSER'S ARGUMENTS AGAINST THE EXPERIENCE OF McTcHANGE

Simon Prosser (2011; 2016) entered the debate with a rather radical claim.[13] Previously, the debate had been whether our experience as of time passing provides perceptual evidence for the passage of time. Our experience is cited as evidence that there is McTchange, and those who deny McTchange have to explain away that appearance as an illusion or anosognosia of some kind. But Prosser claims that not only do we *not* experience time passing, it is impossible that we *could*. Indeed, he argues that the question of time's passing is *unintelligible*. We can't even make sense of the question! He presents two related arguments for this claim, which we will look at now.

ARGUMENT FROM INDISCRIMINABILITY

In his argument from indiscriminability Prosser compares perceptual evidence of time's passing to perceptual evidence of the colour of an object. We can perceive that a tomato is red, but we cannot, in the same sense of 'perceive', perceive that time is passing. He argues that experience doesn't favour views on which time passes (in the metaphysically rich sense discussed in chapter 1) over the view that time does not pass.

In brief Prosser's argument from indiscriminability goes roughly like this:

I1: For perceptual experience to present x as being part of that experience, the brain must be able to act as a *detector* for x.

I2: To act as a detector for x is to have a capacity to discriminate between cases where x is present (or obtains) and cases where x is not present (or does not obtain).

I3: Because time passes whenever a brain is functioning, the brain cannot act discriminate between cases where time passes and cases where time does not pass.

I4: The brain is not a detector for time's passage (from **2** and **3**).

IC. Therefore the passage of time cannot be presented in perceptual experience.

Given that perceptual experience relates us to the world in certain ways, how the world is, ought to make a difference to our experience. If you are looking at a ripe tomato, you have a certain experience, and, typically, if I remove the ripe tomato then experience changes; you are no longer presented in experience with a ripe tomato! The passage of time, Prosser argues, is not like that. It just doesn't make sense to have an experience of time passing, and then to take the passage of time away and see how the experience is different.

ARGUMENT FROM UNINTELLIGIBILITY

Simon Prosser moves from the argument from indiscriminibility to the argument from unintelligibility:

> We cannot experience time as passing, and this undermines our ability to speak or even think about time passing. We do not have any understanding whatsoever of what the world would be like if time passed, for the nature of experience is no guide to this at all.
>
> (Prosser 2016: 55–6)

This picks up a theme from chapter 1; that there is a problem in even so much as explaining what McTchange is. If McTchange isn't a feature of experience, then it is unclear how we could talk about it. If we can't talk about it, then what seemed like the central question of the philosophy of time – 'Is there McTchange?' – isn't really a question at all.

The argument from unintelligibility depends on the argument from indiscriminability. If brains can't detect the passage of time, then we need an explanation of how the people with those brains can talk about it. We can't point at it and say 'look at that time passing!' to tell people what we mean, in the way we can point and say 'look how ripe that tomato is!'.

Not being able to talk about something is a serious problem. If we can't talk about McTchange, we can't have a debate about whether there is such a thing. We would need some other method of pointing out what we meant. We can do this for numbers. The number 2 is the natural number that comes after 1 and before 3, for example. In that case, rather than pointing at something, I've offered a description that can describes something uniquely. There is only 1 natural number higher than 1 and lower than 3.[14]

Prosser thinks that we can offer no such description of the passage of time. If it's meant to be a feature of every possible experience, then how can we distinguish it from other features that are also features of every possible experience? Every possible experience is an experience. Every possible experience is caused in some way. Every possible experience is from a point of view. How do we pick out the passage of time from those other features that belong to every possible experience. I think the answer is that we can contrast time from space, because McTchange over time differs from variation across space. It is by the contrast with space that we can get a grip on what the passage of time is.

IS CHANGE AN ILLUSION?

If we hope to learn whether or not there is McTchange from our experiences of change (or, more specifically, succession), we have a problem. If we have experiences of succession, we could be, as Le Poidevin (2007) argues, *projecting* them onto the world. Or we could be, as Hoerl (2014) argues, under a *cognitive illusion*. We could be convinced that we are experiencing something succession-like, where we simply have no such experience. The illusion is that we *think* we are experiencing something, when there is nothing fitting that description presented in experience. Alternatively, we could simply be failing to say anything intelligible at all. All these words might not mean things after all.

If the hope was that we defend the reality of McTchange because we can point out that we are perceptually aware of McTchange, we meet lots of resistance. We should not give up on experience immediately, however. To begin with, the claim that any experience of succession is simply projected onto the world meets a problem: As P.T. Geach (1969:92) puts the point:

> Even if a man's impressions as to which realities are past, present, and future are illusory, the fact that he has in that case different and uncombinable illusions shows that at least his illusions really are successive – that they are not all present together, but now one illusion is present and now another.

Phillips (2014) makes a similar point in slightly different terms. It's not just that we are perceptually aware of features of time in experience, but our experience itself has temporal structure. Our experience of ripe red tomatoes is not itself ripe or red. But our experience of succession does seem to involve a change in what is presented to us perceptually. This feature of experience is enough to mark time out as special.

Even if we accept that time is special in experience – experience has a successive quality that space does not – this acknowledgement doesn't yet get us to the claim that change is something other than mere temporal variation. It could be something about how we think, or about our biology, that leads us to treat time as special.

It doesn't look like we are going to get a feature of perceptual experience that settles whether there is McTchange. What role does perceptual experience play in establishing the reality of McTchange? If perception is factive, and we really do experience McTchange when we experience qualitative change, movement, lasting, coming to be, ceasing to be, succession, etc. then we do have perceptual evidence for McTchange. But if all those features of perceptual experience are merely experiences of temporal variation from a particular perspective, then we don't have perceptual evidence for McTchange. But simply by observing a ball rolling down a hill, we won't be in a position to tell which account of change from chapter 1 is the correct one! Perceptual experience can give us evidence, without our being able to tell what that evidence is. We have a reason to think that time is special; our experience unfolds in time as well as being experience of various temporal properties. But this doesn't yet give us an explanation of *how* time is special.

QUESTIONS FOR DISCUSSION

1. How do you tell the difference between temporal illusions and temporal anosognosia?
2. Is the flow of time something presented in experience?
3. How does the length of time in a unified experience relate to considerations from the previous chapter?
4. Does our perceptual experience give us reason to think that time is different to (a) colour (b) space?
5. If we have factive perceptual experiences of succession, does that mean that there is McTchange?

NOTES

1 Of course, you can genuinely perceive things that are veridical, but quite limited. You can perceive that there's something in the distance, but misperceive it as a lion, when it is in fact a house next to a tree that looks like a lion from that angle. You are correct that there's something, but not about what it is.

2 John Locke (1690/2004) seems to have held something like this view, which has been very influential. There's a divide about how far the criticisms of the view go. This will re-emerge in the discussion of relationalists and representationalists about perceptual experience later in the chapter.

3 In English law, the 'Gestmin' principles have been influential statements of the unreliability of memory (*Gestmin SGPS SA v Credit Suisse (UK) Ltd & Anor* [2013]):

> in everyday life we are not aware of the extent to which our own and other people's memories are unreliable and believe our memories to be more faithful than they are. Two common (and related) errors are to suppose: (1) that the stronger and more vivid is our feeling or experience of recollection, the more likely the

recollection is to be accurate; and (2) that the more confident another person is in their recollection, the more likely their recollection is to be accurate.

Underlying both these errors is a faulty model of memory as a mental record which is fixed at the time of experience of an event and then fades (more or less slowly) over time. In fact, psychological research has demonstrated that memories are fluid and malleable, being constantly rewritten whenever they are retrieved... External information can intrude into a witness's memory, as can his or her own thoughts and beliefs, and both can cause dramatic changes in recollection. Events can come to be recalled as memories which did not happen at all or which happened to someone else (referred to in the literature as a failure of source memory).

Memory is especially unreliable when it comes to recalling past beliefs. Our memories of past beliefs are revised to make them more consistent with our present beliefs. Studies have also shown that memory is particularly vulnerable to interference and alteration when a person is presented with new information or suggestions about an event in circumstances where his or her memory of it is already weak due to the passage of time.

4 This line of reasoning can be resisted. The idea that perception is our basic relationship with the world, and social dynamics and culture are built on top of it *without affecting it* is a product of a particular view about how perception works.

5 Thomson and Macpherson (2020).

6 There's an interesting question of whether an experience as of movement is also an experience as of not being stationary, or whether we can have experiences that appear to present contradictory properties. As Maurice Merleau-Ponty (1945/2004:6) remarks 'the visual field is that strange zone where contradictory notions jostle each other.'

7 This usage follows Dainton (2011) Hoerl (2013) uses 'intentionalism' rather than 'retentionalism'.

8 See the discussion in chapter 2.

9 E.g. Le Poidevin (2007); Power (2018)

10 See Zahavi (2007) for a discussion of Husserl's views.

11 See Dainton (2022) for an overview.

12 E.g. Van Gelder (1996); Varela (1999); Lloyd (2002); Grush (2007)

13 Hoerl (2014) and Frischhut (2015) have also expressed similar concerns, but Prosser has been the most voluble and prominent on this issue.

14 Obviously we need a way of picking out the number 1 and the number 3. In fact, the Peano axioms give us a way of specifying the structure of the natural numbers that allow us to do this.

FURTHER READING

Deng (2013b) gives an overview of the attempt to explain our experiences as of McTchange.

Dainton (2022) gives an overview of the debate between extentionalists and retentionalists (with various other approaches).

Power (2018) gives a book length attempt to explain experience of time and change, assuming there is no McTchange.

EXPERIENCING THE SELF

If we can't tell whether there is McTchange by looking at clocks, how can we tell? In the previous chapter we suggested that our experience of episodes of time, rather than being spread out in space, was one notable difference between our experience of time and space we need to account for. This chapter is interested in our experience of episodes of time. In particular, it seems like we *last* through episodes of time.

It's not just that it appears that people – in a similar way to tables, mountains, and monarchies – hang around for an extended duration. It's that my experience seems to be an experience of me still being here. I remember being elsewhere, and can imaginatively project myself into the future. My experience seems to be had by a persisting subject – me. In this chapter we'll look at the persistence of a self – yourself – and see how that is connected to how we think about our lives, and how we think about time.

PERSISTENCE

Persistence is the term for being the same through change over time. Questions of persistence are questions of sameness over time and change. If we say that someone persists in speaking, we mean that they continue to speak (usually after something had occurred that would make it difficult, risky, or undesirable to continue). The speaking carries on through a change in situation. In philosophy, we tend to think of *objects* as persisting. This rock continues to be this rock, in spite of being carried from the beach to the garden. We can also think of *subjects* as persisting. That is, we can think that you

DOI: 10.4324/9781003189459-4

can continue to be you through changes in whether you are awake or asleep or through changes in your mood.

There are a host of philosophical questions about what persistence is, and what the persistence conditions of particular objects are. Let's quickly run through three of the main views of what persistence is, so we can get a sense of why it is philosophically puzzling. Then we can get on to thinking about our first-personal awareness as of persistence.

One very natural view of persistence is that there is something that changes, but nonetheless continues to be that very thing. This is how we tend to think about ordinary objects. If I have a notebook, and make some notes in it, it changes, but is still the very same notebook. This is also how we tend to think about people. I get a haircut and go to the gym, I physically change. But, nonetheless, I am the very same person. If someone greets me and says 'you look like a new man!', they don't mean it literally.

Let's call this way of persisting '**endurance**'. If something persists in this way, it endures. Characterising endurance precisely is tricky, since there are competing accounts of how we should do that. For myself, I prefer the account provided by Sally Haslanger (2003): something endures if and only if it is *the proper subject of change*. That is the enduring thing must be the kind of thing that we properly describe as changing, where it continues to be that thing both before and after the change.

This definition makes more sense if we contrast it with two other accounts of persistence. **Perdurance** is the way of persisting where something has different temporal parts that differ from one another. We might think of events in this way; we could say that the party has a tense initial phase, but then is more relaxed once the dancing begins. Why is this not the proper subject of change? Well, the thought here is that the different temporal parts of party are changes, but we shouldn't describe the *party* as changing, merely as having different temporal parts which differ.[1] The party, on this view, is made up of different temporal parts in sequence, and doesn't change what parts it has, or what sequence they are in. You can see the attraction that this view might have for someone who denies that there is McTchange, since it treats persistence as temporal variation across an object composed of temporal parts. But although this affinity has been noted,[2] others have both denied McTchange and defended endurance as a way things persist.[3] It's also worth mentioning that someone who accepts notebooks endure though change can also accept that parties perdure. The '*endurantist*' is usually understood to be someone committed to *some* things enduring, not committed to the claim that everything does.

The contrast between perdurance and endurance is useful for understanding them. Perdurance is the view that persisting objects are made up of different parts at different times, in the same kind of way that extended objects are made up of different parts in different places. Perduring objects are – and this is genuinely the correct technical term – 'four-dimensional space-time worms'. That is, when we represent them in a physicist's four-dimensional diagram, they look like long, thin, wriggly worms. Endurantism, by contrast, claims that objects are not spread out over time the way they are spread out over space. Sometimes this thought is put as being that they are 'wholly present' at each time they exist.[4] So, we don't say *part* of my notebook is in my bag, but just that my notebook is. This helps us see the difference between the notebook being the proper subject of change (the notebook changes from being in my bag to being in my hand) and the claim that it has parts in my bag and parts in my hand.

The third view of persistence we should discuss is **exdurance**. Rather than thinking of objects or events as *made up of* temporal parts, on *exdurantism*, the objects or events *are* the temporal parts. On *perdurantism*, as we have seen, objects are space-time worms, but on exdurantism they are stages, or time-slices. Strictly speaking, exduring objects don't change; they are momentary time-slices that form part of a sequence of such time-slices. The idea is that a momentary time-slice is related to other time-slices by 'counterpart' relations. Basically, you get the sequence by looking for similarity and causal relations.[5] This, according to its defenders, gets you the best of both worlds. You get the contrast between being 'wholly present' at a time (which the exdurantist time-slices literally are), and being spread out across space. But you also avoid the big worry about enduring objects – that they change.

The problem of change is that change appears to require that things have different properties to themselves. The notepad is empty at one time, and full at another. But if it is *the very same* notepad, it ought to have a single consistent set of properties. This is because of a principle known as *the indiscernibility of identicals*. If something is identical to itself, it should have all the same properties as itself.[6] But precisely what it is to be the proper subject of change is to be the very same thing through change in properties.

There are various responses to the problem of change, but exdurantism is one where you deny that things change their properties. Persisting through change is a matter of standing in the right relationships to a sequence of suitably varied counterparts. If you aren't inclined toward exdurantism, the endurantist has a number of technical responses involving claims about what it is to have a property. Perhaps my notebook isn't in my bag, but in-my-bag-at-time-*t*, or perhaps the *way* my notebook has a property is different at different times. The endurantist might say, for example that the notebook is in my bag 10am-ly, and out of my bag 10.15-ly. Just as quickly and cheaply are ways of something happening, 10am-ly is a way of being in in my bag.

My own response is to think that change in properties avoids the 'problem of change' if it is McTchange of properties. Changing properties just is what enduring objects do. The logical difficulties here are just a feature of things changing over time rather than being spread out like they are across space.[7] Though I should warn readers that my response may be a little controversial amongst participants in this debate. They might describe this position as 'ostrich-endurantism', since it simply avoids accepting there is a problem, and so figuratively involves burying one's head in the sand as ostriches proverbially do.

FIRST-PERSONAL EXPERIENCE OF PERSISTENCE

Questions of persistence can apply to anything. They are particularly interesting when we apply them to ourselves. When we reflect on our experience, we notice that we seem to last through time, rather than feel as though we are spread out across it. Lying in bed, I can stretch out like a starfish, but I simply can't stretch out across the night in the same way.

When we project ourselves into the future, we can do so in different ways. You can narrate a story in which you appear as a named character, for example, and you can imagine the adventures of that character, without necessarily thinking of that character as being *you*. Or you could picture yourself doing various things, as if seen by someone else. Or you could imagine *being* the person doing some activity. As L.A. Paul (2017:266) argues, when we project ourselves into the near future, we tend to adopt the first-personal perspective – we imagine *being* the person doing whatever we're imagining – but the further into the future the less we tend to imagine first-personally in this way.[8]

When we project ourselves into the future as being the person who is in the future, it seems we are imaginatively treating ourselves as *enduring*. That doesn't establish that endurance is the correct account of persistence for us, but it does suggest that we naturally presuppose it as an account of persistence.

SCEPTICISM ABOUT THE SELF

Suppose we accept what we experience does suggest that we experience lasting through time differently to taking up space. One response is to deny that there is anything to persist. We could deny that there are *selves* to persist through time at all.

David Hume, the 18th century philosopher of the Scottish Enlightenment, argued that we were unable to observe something – *the self* – doing the experiencing, just the sequence of experiences themselves. 'Selves' seem to be an invention to make sense of experiences coming in sequences.

This worry that we have invented selves gets picked up by Derek Parfit (1984:281). He described feelings of liberation, and of consolation, once he came to reject the idea that there is a self that he needs to care about the survival of.

> When I believed that my existence was a further fact, I seemed imprisoned in myself. My life seemed like a glass tunnel, through which I was moving faster every year, and at the end of which there was darkness. When I changed my view, the walls of my glass tunnel disappeared. I now live in the open air. There is still a difference between my life and the lives of other people. But the difference is less. I am less concerned about the rest of my own life, and more concerned about the lives of others.

This connection between our moral attitudes and our belief in the persistence of the self is going to become pretty important. For one thing, it shows a connection between the debate about persistence, and the reason to care about it; how we project ourselves into the future affects how we act in the future and how we treat ourselves and other people.

Parfit was an exdurantist. He believed that persistence was a matter of standing in a certain relation – the 'R' relation – to past or future counterparts.[9] The sense of liberation comes from realising the future experiences you project yourself into are not really yours, and don't have more moral significance than the ones other people project themselves into. We each project ourselves into these ones because they are similar to our own, and we might be able to influence them more easily (since we are causally related to them), but it's not that we should care more for those counterparts we are 'R' related to than for other time-slices of people, it's just that it's practically easier to affect them.

J. David Velleman (2006:3) notes a similarity between Parfit's views and those of 'the Buddhists'. Both think we can be relieved from suffering by overcoming the idea that we are enduring selves. The burden of worrying about our future well-being can be removed by ceasing to think of there being an 'us' in the future. But Velleman also remarks on a dissimilarity. Parfit thought that you can be persuaded of the non-existence of the self by reading his book, whereas Buddhists think years of meditation, training and practice are required to 'extinguish' the self. Certainly, I think the tendency to project ourselves into the past and future is very strong, so it would be no surprise that it would be a difficult tendency to overcome. But the central question that we will return to is whether overcoming this is desirable. Before we get on to that, let's spend a while understanding what 'the Buddhists' think about persistence of selves.

THE BUDDHIST NOT-SELF THESIS

Buddhist philosophy arises out of a series of philosophical/religious debates in Classical India during the 5th century BC.[10] Much of the terminology of Buddhist philosophy is in common with Indian traditions which evolved into what we would now call Hinduism. Buddhism splits into different traditions itself. *Theravada Buddhism* the oldest of the surviving traditions, has key texts written in Pali, and is widely practiced in Sri Lanka, Thailand, Cambodia, Laos and Burma (Myanmar). *Mahayana Buddhism* has its key texts written in Sanskrit, and is widely practiced in Vietnam, Malaysia, Nepal, China, Korea, Japan, and Bhutan.[11]

Although these various Buddhist traditions all follow the teachings of the Buddha, this allows lots of room for interpretation and debate, over more than two millennia. This means that we need to be incredibly cautious about claiming a view as 'The Buddhist view'.[12] The central teachings which they all have in common are reasonably easy to summarise (if not quite as easy to grasp).

THE THREE MARKS OF EXISTENCE

- **Impermanence** (Pali '*anicca*'; Sanskrit '*anitya*')
- **Unsatisfactoriness** (Pali '*dukkha*'; Sanskrit '*duhkha*')
- **Not-Self** (Palai '*anatta*'; Sanskrit '*anatman*')

Impermanence is a commitment to change. All the things we encounter are in a state of change from one form to another. Periods of stability are misleading exceptions, whereas things are really constantly in flux.

Unsatisfactoriness (sometimes translated as 'suffering') arises from our resistance to change. We want to cling on to the fleeting and the impermanent, and doing so is impossible.

Not-Self is naturally the mark of existence that Velleman and Parfit see as related to debates about endurantism. A note of caution, however, is that the contrast here is with a permanent essence to a person/living being that survived all change and can survive reincarnation. The rejection of the self is a rejection of an *unchanging essence*. In the previous section, the endurantist seemed to be subject to criticism for accepting that selves persist through change. That is, the endurantist position is that there is a *changing* self.[13] So, it may well be that some versions of the 'not-self' view are compatible with the commitment to endurantism.

THE FOUR NOBLE TRUTHS

The link between relieving suffering and rejecting suffering is made explicit in the 'Four Noble Truths':[14]

1. There is unsatisfactoriness ('*dukkha*'/'*duhkha*') in the kinds of lives that humans normally lead.
2. Unsatisfactoriness arises from desire of various kinds, including craving for food, sex and drugs, craving for status, and craving for security and immortality.

3. Overcoming unsatisfactoriness is possible (and desirable), by no longer desiring those things (and not desiring the desires for those things).
4. The route to overcoming unsatisfactoriness is given in the *Eightfold Path*.[15]

So, we've got three marks of existence, and four noble truths, the last of which is an eight-step path to enlightenment. The use of numbered lists is presumably designed to help people memorise the various elements. In the original languages, they would have used other features, such as rhyme and assonance to make them more memorable still.

I won't go into the Eightfold Path here, but let's pause for a moment to reflect on the picture that is emerging. The way that most people live involves them having desires that are fundamentally unsatisfiable. The aim is to *overcome* the normal human condition, with the unsatisfiable desires that arise out of it, by coming to accept *in the way we live, work and think* that these desires do not need to be satisfied. Many of these desires arise because we are committed to projecting ourselves into the past and future. We care what happens to *us* in a way that makes us scared that we have something to lose, and that we should secure things for ourselves that other people also need. It is this caring about ourselves and our desires at the expense of others that we must overcome. We are supposed to achieve this by overcoming, in the way we live, work and think, the distinction between ourself and others.

THE NOT-SELF THESIS

It's not clear that what denying the existence of a self amounts to. As I have said, the denial of an eternal, unchanging self that has a fixed essence doesn't obviously require denying endurantism as I have outlined it. There is some difference between denying that the person who orders a cup of coffee and the person who picks it up can be literally the same person and the denial of an immortal soul.

Indeed, this debate is one that has taken place *within* Buddhism. The '*Pudgalavada*' view was the view that there is some minimal sense in which a person endures. Amber Carpenter (2014:32) describes the view like this:

> It [the self] is, perhaps, a bit of metaphysical glue, making it possible for us to re-identify the same person over time and through change; it is perhaps a bit of psychological glue, preventing us falling off the steep precipice into nihilism. If the continuity between different psychological events is real… then the self must be equally real, for it just is this continuity.

This is a minority view within Buddhism, but it tells you something about how radical the Not-Self thesis potentially is. Non-Buddhists often object to the 'Not-Self' thesis for being incompatible with agency and moral responsibility. Philosophers of the Nyaya Hindu school, for example, defend what was the Classical Indian common-sense position. As Dasti and Bryant (2013:5–6) put it:

> Nyāya philosophers agree that the enduring individual self must be the locus of agency and moral responsibility, and correspondingly attack Buddhist no-self theories. They argue that rejection of an enduring self makes it impossible to explain moral responsibility over time: if there is no enduring self, I am not the same individual that I was last week, or, for that matter, in my previous birth. This disassociation, Nyāya argues, would make me free of moral responsibility for what 'he' did back then as much as I am currently not responsible for what my neighbo[u]r does right now.

Having urged caution about wading into Classical Indian Philosophy, I am now going to say something incautious. There are moves in these Classical Indian Debates that look like they could be at home in contemporary English-language philosophy journals. Despite the complexity of these traditions, and some stuff that looks alien to a scientific world-view (such as the focus on reincarnation), lots of the thinking is strikingly recognisable.

It is very tempting to read Parfit as agreeing quite closely with particular Buddhist views. Yogacara Buddhist philosophers, such as Vasubandhu, engage very clearly with a view where we can only make sense of memory by appealing to an enduring self. As Perrett (2016:186) explains:

> Vasubandhu rejects such an account of memory as being possible only if there is a continuously existing substance that both had the experience and is now remembering it. Instead he analyses a person as being a series of causally related momentary person-stages, with memory the result of a chain of momentary impressions[16]... occurring in a series of person-stages.

Vasubanadhu seems to be defending exdurantism some 16 centuries before Derek Parfit!

There are two key claims here to focus on:

The Radical Claim: The way we ordinarily live/think needs to be overcome.

The Non-Enduring Claim: We must reject endurance as an account of our own persistence through change.

We have seen that accepting the Not-Self thesis doesn't quite amount to accepting the Non-Enduring Claim. I leave as an open question, whether the Radical Claim is true. But the Buddhist argument for the Non-Enduring Claim (amongst the Buddhists who accept it) will depend on accepting the Radical Claim. The debate about time has got us thinking about fundamental questions of how humans ought to live.[17]

We got into Buddhist philosophy because we were thinking about reasons to reject the idea that we have reason to believe in McTchange, because we experience ourselves as enduring through change (and enduring through change is best explained by appeal to McTchange). Buddhism was appealed to because there are versions of Buddhism that reject the enduring self. But note that Impermanence was one of the marks of existence. That might be taken to be supportive of McTchange. The argument for rejecting the first-personal enduring self might itself presuppose McTchange! Even here we find different views. Some Buddhists, like the Sautrantikas and Theravadins, are more clearly committed to McTchange, whereas others, like Nagarjuna (150–250 CE) can be read as thinking of change as being a fiction, or a mere appearance, or a mere way of talking.[18]

What have we gained from this section? For one thing, we have acknowledged that these debates aren't exclusive to Western philosophical traditions. This might help persuade you that whether or not there is McTchange is a question that we could arrive at even if we didn't start with philosophical debates in Cambridge in the early 20th century. For another thing we have been reminded that philosophy is very demanding. If we ignore historical debates (especially in other languages), we often end up reinventing them. But if we do engage with them, they turn out to be as complex and difficult as the ones we started with.

It remains the case that many millions of people belong to traditions that embrace the Radical Claim, and take it to mean that we should accept the Non-Enduring Claim.[19] In the next section we will look at the case for thinking that we need the enduring self to make sense of moral responsibility and agency.

SPECIAL CONCERN FOR OUR FUTURE SELVES

We project ourself into the future, partly, it seems, because we care about what happens to us in a way that we don't care about most other people. Perhaps this is a problem we must overcome. But it seems like there are reasons to care for ourselves in the future that don't apply to other people. This might be because the way we relate to our future self is very different from our relation to other people. We can control what happens to our future self, for example, by taking action that affects our future now.[20]

Much of this can be accepted by the exdurantist. They think current time-slices have future counterparts because of the similarity and causal connectedness of those time-slices. The endurantist needs something *more*. Susan Wolf (1986:709) offers the following thought:

> If the reason we care about persons is that persons are able to live interesting, admirable, and rewarding lives, we may answer that time slices of persons, much less experiences of time slices, are incapable of living lives at all.

The objection to viewing the self as a time-slice that stands in counterpart relations to other time-slices is that we can only make sense of people as acting over a period of time. The problem isn't merely of identifying which time-slices to care about, but of making sense of people as momentary time-slices.[21]

Suppose you are making a cup of tea. In carrying out that aim, there are various steps that you need to take. These will involve paying attention to what you are doing. If you don't pay attention boiling water ends up in the wrong place. It's not that we need to relate the time-slice that wants a cup of tea to the time-slice that has a cup of tea (and the desire for a cup of tea satisfied). It's that *intending* to make a cup of tea isn't a thought that you can have instantaneously at the start that gets satisfied later, but something that you enact throughout the making of the tea. What you are doing (and intending to do) at a moment makes sense in terms of activities you are in the midst of, rather than the activities being built up of momentary states, intentions or desires. That, at least, is the argument as to why we should think of persons as not being exdurantist.

Christine Korsgaard (1989:113–4) puts the point forcefully:

> To ask why the present self should cooperate with the future ones is to assume that the present self has reasons with which it already identifies, and which are independent of those later selves…to the extent that you regulate your choices by identifying yourself as the one who is implementing something like a particular plan of life, you need to identify with your future in order to *be what you are even now*.

We need to think of ourselves as enduring through change because we can only make sense of agency if plans are things we are around long enough to carry out. In some cases of plans, like crossing the road or making tea for ourselves, we assume that we'll be around for the whole plan. Other plans we might hope that someone will take up after us. In fact, we often set up organisations or institutions that can endure through change to make long-term plans happen, because then the organisation can be around long enough to carry out the whole plan.

THE UNITY OF AGENCY

If we need the 'metaphysical glue' of persisting through time to make sense of agency, it is worth thinking a little about what agency requires. The argument that we need the self to endure – to be the proper subject of change – is that we need something that is around throughout the change. That is, agency requires *unity of agency*.

Unity of agency comes in two forms: unity at a time and unity over time. Unity at a time is useful because there needs to be some kind of resultant effect produced from amongst one's various desires, intentions etc. Agency requires that the goals and desires that one starts with lead to action (and that that action isn't self-defeating). There are lots of examples where agency is made up of independent actions that are not always entirely consistent with one another. The octopus has arms that seem to act intelligently somewhat independently of one another.[22] Some experiments on so-called 'split-brain' patients, where the *corpus callosum* has been severed, reveal phenomena where the two hemispheres of the human brain seem to act independently of one another.[23] And group agents, like families, parliaments, musical ensembles, businesses and governments can still carry out actions in spite of some differences in the aims of the individuals making them up.

Acting nonetheless requires that there is some action that results, even if the agent exhibits some inner conflict. Plans might be carried out inefficiently by disunified agents, and the agents may change their minds. But there is an important difference between a consistent plan that is badly carried out, and an inconsistent plan which cannot be carried out at all. *Some* action might take place, but whatever happens won't in fact have inconsistent properties.

Unity over time interests us most in this section. The requirement that agency must involve unity over time is central to the argument that we need to think of ourselves as enduring through change to make sense of agency. Unity of agency over time is exactly the requirement that the agent is around throughout the action. The consequences of the action may carry on long after the action has been finished. But part of what makes an action the action that it is will be that there is a single guiding intention that makes the different bits of the action intelligible, monitors the action to make sure it is going as intended and unites the different bits of the action together as a single big action.

FROM AGENCY TO McTcHANGE

We began this chapter wondering why we might think that there is McTchange, if we couldn't tell by looking at clocks. The thought with which we began was that there is some interesting difference between our experience of lasting through time and our experience of being spread out across space. This contrast between the way we experience ourselves through time and across space seems to be where the idea that change might be different from temporal variation comes from.

We considered three different accounts of persistence: endurantism, perdurantism, and exdurantism, and identified that endurantism might be a view that requires us to accept McTchange. This is one of the first places that the appeal to McTchange might be resisted. You could argue that we do persist by enduring, but that doesn't commit us to McTchange.

We then considered a second place where the appeal to McTchange might be resisted. It might be that the *appearance* of our persisting by enduring is a habit of thought that we must overcome. Indeed, on this view such a habit of thought is responsible for selfishness, and we can overcome selfishness if we overcome the commitment to an enduring self. We spent a while considering the rejection of the self found in Buddhist philosophies. We noted that it makes a difference:

- what we mean by the self (we need no commitment to reincarnation to accept the enduring self),
- why we think that we should reject the self (accepting that everything is constantly changing seems to presuppose McTchange), and
- whether we think overcoming selfishness is really what's good for creatures like us.

Finally, we considered a reason why having enduring selves might be useful. They provide a 'metaphysical glue' that allows us to be coherent agents over time. We need to think of ourselves as enduring through time because we can't make sense of agents as built up from time-slices in a sequence.

This appeal to our first-personal experience seems to provide the strongest case for McTchange. But the case gives us reasons why it might be *helpful* if there is McTchange. It might be that we would be better abandoning the idea of persisting through change, and training ourselves out of selfishness. And it might be that we wouldn't be able to make sense of human agency if we abandoned the idea of persisting through change. But someone could reply: 'so much the worse for human agency!'. At best the argument from our experience of persisting through change is going to give us support for a working hypothesis that there is McTchange which we *hope* is right. The support for it will not come from direct evidence in experience, but from the extent to which adopting the hypothesis allows us to make sense of the world. If this hypothesis conflicts with empirical evidence from science, then it will be in trouble.

QUESTIONS FOR DISCUSSION

1. How far in the future do you still imagine the world as seen from your perspective?
2. Why can't one thing have incompatible properties at different times?
3. Would you be happier if you stopped caring for your future in a different way to other people's future?
4. Can there be actions with agents that are not unified over time?
5. Does your experience of lasting over time give you reason to think there is McTchange?

NOTES

1 I don't think this sounds right. We can say that the party changed, it seems to me. But this is meant to be the sort of example that makes perdurance seem intuitive.
2 Sider (2001)
3 Mellor (1998)
4 Mark Johnston (1984) was responsible for this formulation in terms of being 'wholly present', which was then popularised by David Lewis (1986). Johnston (2011:52 fn36) thinks the phrase has become unhelpful, and that talk of enduring entities as being 'wholly present'

> should stop; for given this account of endurance, it is quite unclear how a variably constituted entity, one that is capable of gaining and losing parts, can even be a candidate to be an enduring entity. (Are all of the parts it has over time to be present at each time? Of course not! But then which parts are to be wholly present at each time?) Yet many enduring substances are variably constituted.

5 Note here that you are building up sequences out of moments, which brings in some of the discussions from chapter 2.

6 Identity is a very unusual relation, because it is a relation that something can only have to itself. If you have two things, they cannot be identical to each other, precisely because there are two of them. Identity is a matter of being one and the same thing. There is a colloquial sense of 'identity' where two things are said to be identical. Technically, we would say these things are 'exactly similar'.

7 The difficulties, in my opinion, are more-or-less the same difficulties discussed in chapter 1. The problem of change is closely related to McTaggart's argument for the unreality of time.

8 Baron, Latham, Miller, Oh (MS) argue that it is far from clear that we do naturally presuppose such a view. I take it that the contrast between our experience of extension in space and succession of time is quite robust, but how we conceptualise this contrast is more highly variable.

9 The 'R' stands for 'relation'.

10 The Buddha is roughly a contemporary of Zeno, who we discussed in chapter 2. There's an open question about why Indian philosophy, Greek philosophy, and also Chinese philosophy, had such significant periods around the same time. Given archaeological evidence of trade in material goods across continents, there's also a question about how much mutual influence there was between thinkers during this period.

11 So, as a rule of thumb, if you see terms untranslated from Pali, that's a sign you're discussing Theravada Buddhism, and untranslated terms from Sanskrit indicates Mahayana Buddhism. These traditions themselves branched off to form new ones. *Vajrayana* Buddhism, commonly practiced in Tibet, is sometimes considered an offshoot of Mahayana Buddhism, and sometimes considered its own tradition. Mahayana Tradition has all the same key texts as Theravada Buddhism, plus others, and in general is characterised by a willingness to reframe the key points of Buddhism to suit the context and the audience. This explains why it often gets combined with other traditions, such as Daoism, to create distinctive forms of Buddhist practice such as Japanese Zen Buddhism.

12 Imagine talking about a Christian view, where you are trying to generalise over the Syriac Orthodox Church, the Westboro Baptist Church, and the Quakers, plus everything in between.

13 Velleman acknowledges that he is not a scholar of Buddhism, and I cannot claim to be either. It is good that this bridge between analytic philosophy and Classical Indian philosophy has been made. But it is worth noting how much *richer* the contributions of Buddhist philosophy are than the superficial similarity to Parfit's views suggest.

14 This has become the standard translation, though more accurately it might be that the ones who know the truths that are noble, rather than the truths themselves.

15 The eightfold path can be summarised as follows: right view, right aspiration, right speech, right action, right livelihood, right effort, right mindfulness, right concentration. Of course, each of these requires considerable interpretation themselves. But note that there are readings on which you can't overcome unsatisfactoriness unless you live the life of a Buddhist monk. Reading Parfit's book *Reasons and Persons* isn't going to be enough!

16 Vāsanās (Sanskrit)

17 This will happen again. But also, we'll be discussing physics again soon. Philosophy of Time really covers a lot of ground.

18 See Miller (2017) for discussion.

19 Many non-Buddhist ethical worldviews will endorse the Radical Claim. Epicureanism, for example, claims that we must overcome unsatisfiable desires to relieve suffering. But they have notably different views of time, for example.

20 It looks like there are lots of cases where we care about other people where we don't have control over them, but care about them in a way we don't for other people generally. Romantic partners, children, parents, siblings, close friends, for example, may be subject to such a special concern for the future. One potential explanation for this is that there is a group agent that we belong to – an *us* – that we have special concern for.

21 The themes of chapter 2 are coming through again here.

22 Godfrey-Smith (2018)

23 Nagel (1971)

FURTHER READING

Paul (2017) examines our first-personal experience as of enduring.

Hawley (2001) argues for exdurantism, but chapter 1 gives an excellent introduction to the problem of change.

Velleman (2006) argues that endurantism is incoherent and there are ethical benefits to overcoming it.

Miller (2017) gives an outline of the relationship between Buddhist views and Western views of time.

RELATIVITY OF SIMULTANEITY

Most physicists reject McTchange. They do so for two reasons. One is because they think that they can explain everything they need to in terms of mere temporal variation.[1] The other is because they often take the *Theory of Relativity* to be in conflict with McTchange. In this chapter we'll outline some of the issues in physics that have bearing on the debate about whether there is McTchange, and look at the options that that debate leaves open. We'll be rejecting the view that there is incompatibility between the Theory of Relativity and McTchange. Nonetheless, the Theory of Relativity forces a response from defenders of McTchange.

GALILEAN RELATIVITY

What do we mean by 'Relativity'? There is quite a lot of scene-setting to do to get to the Theory of Relativity, so we'll start with the idea of relative motion. Imagine you are lying down in a room with no windows. You don't feel anything moving. The furniture in the room, the glass of water on the desk, the lamp hanging from the ceiling; they are all perfectly still. You aren't moving either. You are lying there just contemplating the stillness. We have established that the furniture isn't moving *relative to the room*, that the water isn't moving *relative to the glass* and the lamp is not moving *relative to the ceiling*. When we are claiming that something is moving, we are always making that claim relative to something else.

Let's say the room, the furniture, the glass of water and the light hanging from the ceiling all share an *inertial frame*. That is just to say that they aren't moving relative to each other and that nothing is

DOI: 10.4324/9781003189459-5

accelarating. An inertial frame is useful, because we can measure things as moving *relative to it*. Galilean Relativity is the sort of relativity we have just observed: that we can measure motion relative to an inertial frame. The laws of motion work the same, regardless of which inertial frame you use.

As Galileo Galilei pointed out, if you are in such a room, you can't tell whether the room itself is moving or not. You could tell if it was *accelerating*, but not if it is moving at constant speed. You would need to be able to compare it to something you already knew was not moving – 'at rest' – in order to establish whether or not it was moving. Galileo asked to imagine a room in a ship, where nothing in the room is moving relative to anything else, but the ship is moving relative to the dock outside.

Spoiler: There's not going to turn out to be anything we already know is at rest.

THE NEWTONIAN PICTURE OF SPACE AND TIME

During the 17th century, the picture of the world that leading thinkers worked with underwent a significant change. While the Ancient Greeks were using mathematical concepts to think about space and time, the 17th century started to see a scientific theory based on precise measurement and testable observations. Isaac Newton is associated with a picture of space and time that was the basis of physical approaches until the early 20th century. Other figures besides Newton, most notably Gottfried Leibniz, contributed hugely to ongoing philosophical debates about what time was, and how the maths related to the world it attempted to describe. But Newton's influence was so significant, his name tends to be the one we associate with those 17th century developments.

The picture we get from Newton is that space has three dimensions, which obey the postulates of *Euclidean Geometry,* and time is another dimension, which flows continuously in a single direction. The three dimensions of space are infinite, and time will continue infinitely. Time, on this view, is unaffected by what is going on in time, or which bit of space it is going on in. Time and space are *absolute*, in Newtonian physics. That is to say that there is an objective fact about what is at rest, and it is relative to that objectively resting inertial frame that absolute motion can be measured.

Newtonian physics also has no privileged places or times. Newton's laws of motion apply always, everywhere, to all matter.

EUCLIDEAN GEOMETRY

One Ancient Greek legacy of Newton's picture of space and time was that space has a *metric*. That is, we can perform transformations on shapes that preserve continuities, corners, angles and distances. The metric provided by Euclidean geometry gives us results such as the sum of the interior angles of any triangle equals two right angles. Euclidean geometry gets used a lot in real-life engineering contexts, but the differences between the geometry of Newtonian space and time and the geometry of the Universe we actually find ourself in will be crucial for understanding why contemporary physics appears to create issues for McTchange. So, let's think carefully about what Euclidean geometry involves.

For a start let's consider the tools that Euclidean geometry relies on:

- The pencil
- The straightedge
- The pair of compasses

Euclidean geometry describes what you can do with those three tools in combination.

To begin with the pencil: you can draw lines with a pencil. The type of geometrical structure that pencils get you is called a *topology*. It describes whether lines are connected to each other or not. That is, it describes continuity. A piece of string has the same topology if you tie it in a knot, but two pieces of string are topologically different to each other even if you knot them together. So a topology allows for all sorts of deformations because it is just that bit of geometrical structure concerned with continuity or discontinuity. Topology doesn't treat straight lines differently to curved lines, it doesn't preserve distances, and it doesn't distinguish between corners and curves. But topology *does* preserve intersections of lines, shapes being inside other shapes or outside them and holes in shapes.

The pencil can be combined with a straightedge, which allows you to draw *straight* lines. This gets you an additional level of structure: *affine* structure. Affine structure preserves straightness as well as topology. In Euclidean geometry, you can draw a straight line between any two points, and you can extend any finite straight line continuously in a straight line. Indeed, every pair of points are the endpoints of exactly one straight line. But we don't have any information about angles or distances yet. So, we can stretch shapes as we like in an affine structure, provided all the straight lines stay straight. This is why the tool we used was a straightedge and not a ruler; the ruler has a marked scale, and the straight edge doesn't.

To get distances and angles we need our third piece of equipment, the pair of compasses. What the pair of compasses allow us to do is inscribe circles. Circles are special because they are lines that are the *same distance* from a particular point. So, in Euclidean space, a complete closed circle can be drawn around any point for any distance from that point. Once we have circles and points, and straight lines between those points, we have the resources to measure angles and distances; we get a distinction between squares and rectangles, equilateral triangles and right-angled triangles, and we get distances, where 10 units in one direction is the same as 10 units in another. That is, we get a *metric* on space. This means that we can rotate shapes while preserving the intersections, the corners, the straight lines, and the angles and distances between them. This is *incredibly useful*.

Newton thought that, at every moment in time, space had a Euclidean geometry, and that the points of space persisted though time. So something could be located *at the very same point* in space for a period of time. To be moving is to occupy *different points of space* and to be at rest is to be occupying *the same* points.

In addition to a distinction between moving or not moving, Newton has a concept of *uniform* motion. So we can make sense of changing place *at a constant rate*. So if you move 10 miles an hour for two miles, not only are the 20 miles all equally a mile long, but each hour is equally 1 hour long. In addition to the three-dimensions of space having a metrical structure, the one dimension of time does too.[2] This metrical structure not only gives us fixed intervals between events, but ratios between them. Each hour is the same length, and two hours is twice as long as one hour. Newton's views of space and time were revolutionary because they led him to develop mathematically precise laws of motion, which enabled much more precise measurements to be taken and the improved ability to predict and control mechanical devices allowed for the development of precision engineering.[3]

RELATIVITY OF SIMULTANEITY

The problems with relativity begin with the realisation that we have no means of identifying what are the *same* points of space and what are different points. We can't work out what is absolutely at rest and what isn't. It might seem that your house is in the same place it was yesterday. But that is only if we treat the ground as at rest. But the Earth is spinning on its axis, and orbiting the sun, and the sun is moving relative to the rest of the galaxy, which is moving relative to other galaxies. If these things are moving, they are occupying *different* bits of space. But to identify something as occupying the *same* bit of space we need something that is objectively not moving to compare it to. And we don't have anything. Galilean Relativity is the best that we can do. Nonetheless, we might pick an inertial frame that is the most useful for most of our purposes. This seemed like a really good plan. Except something unexpected happened.

THE MICHELSON–MORLEY EXPERIMENT

Here's an idea for an experiment. Shine a light in two directions; one in the direction of travel and the other off to the side. Arrange things so the light will be reflected back at you from a certain distance. The time it takes for the light to complete this trip, the pre-relativistic theory predicts, should be different depending on whether it is in the direction you are travelling or not – in one direction you give extra speed to the light and in the other you don't. So *if you don't know which direction you are moving in,* you can use this set-up to work out in which direction you (and your laboratory) are moving. This was the idea behind the Michelson–Morley experiment. (See figure 5.1.)

The experiment assumes that it is conducted in an inertial frame (acceleration would produce different effects). By getting the light signals to produce interference patterns it's possible to measure the time that the light took for the round trip very accurately. But they

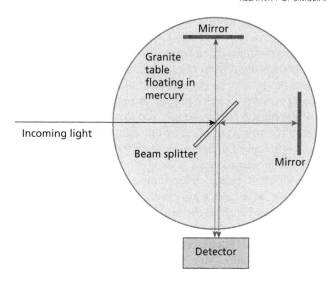

Figure 5.1 The Michelson–Morley experiment

found the speed of light was the same in all directions. This was a bad result for pre-relativistic physics.

What's so startling about the Michelson–Morley experiment? What does it do that Galilean Relativity can't handle? Galilean Relativity says that how fast something appears to be moving will vary depending on how fast the observer is moving. But light, it turns out, doesn't work like that. Light has the same maximum speed (in a vacuum, where there's nothing to slow it down) regardless of which inertial frame you are in. And it's not just light. The top speed possible for any type of signal is the same regardless of what inertial frame you are in. If what we were interested in was not light as such but information, or causal influence, what would matter is whatever means could let us send the fastest signal. But there's no way to send information at faster than the speed of light, whether it's by carrier pigeon, e-mail, semaphore or telepathy.

Think about the fact that we don't all share an inertial frame. Suppose you are lying in bed, and I am on a speeding rocket. From our point of view, the top speed that we can send information is the same, but we are going at different speeds relative to one another. What the Michelson–Morley experiment showed was that if I send a light signal while already moving quickly, it doesn't affect the speed of the signal for you. I don't catch up with it, but neither does it appear to you to be going faster than a signal you sent. We can't add the speed of light from my perspective to the speed I'm going from your perspective to get the speed of my light from your perspective. If it were a carrier pigeon, we could take my speed, the speed of the pigeon relative to me, and then work out the speed of the pigeon for you. Regardless of our different relative speeds, the top speed – the speed of light – from each of our perspectives is the same (i.e. 'frame-invariant).

From different perspectives things appear differently. What appears to be a sequence of events happening in order to me might appear to be all at the same time to you. That the fastest signal we can send is 'frame-invariant' has consequences for how we measure things. If the speed of light is what is constant between different inertial frames, the lengths and durations of things won't be. They'll differ relative to the speed of light. Some things in a different inertial frame will be squashed in space and time and other things stretched, compared to what they would be like within that inertial frame.

Physicists use the term 'foliation' for splitting the Universe up into a sequence of events, one after the other. Think of a big book with pages that sequentially represent moments in time. Different inertial frames will provide different foliations. In the absence of an account about which inertial frame is 'really' at rest, there is no unique foliation of the Universe that we can extract from the physics in a principled way. Rival foliations will have some events in different orders to each other. That is, without a way of specifying what perspective the information on each page of the big book should be based on, we have no way to work out how to split it into separate pages that gives events a definitive order.

SPACE–TIME

One result of the move to relativistic physics is that what is at the same time as what depends on which inertial frame you use to create your coordinate system. In fact, we need to stop treating time as a single dimension in addition to the three Euclidean dimensions in Newton's theory. We end up instead with a 'four-dimensional manifold' that involves three space-like directions and a time-like direction. That is, we can no longer treat time separately from space.

It is not, let's be clear, that there is no difference between space and time when dealing with space–time. We're not in danger of turning at a funny angle and starting to age sideways! But the things we can say are somewhat reduced. If we have received a signal from somewhere, we can safely say that it's in our past. Because light goes as fast as any signal can, the region of the Universe that you could possibly receive a signal from is called your '*past light-cone*'. And the corresponding region that you could possibly send a signal to is called your '*future light-cone*'. These regions represent the things that are *time-like* separated from you. The area that is neither in your past light-cone nor future light-cone is *space-like* separated from you, in a region we can call '*absolute elsewhere*'. (See figure 5.2.) But your future light cone might contain a different region of the Universe from someone else travelling at a very different speed to you. You won't necessarily be able to agree with other observers about what's in the future, what's in the past, and what is going on *right now*.

One of the key features of space–time is that there is *relativity of simultaneity*. That means that you might appear to do something at the same time as me, without my appearing to do something at the same time as you. Normally we think being the 'same as' is *transitive* and *symmetric*. That means if *x* is the same as *y*, and *y* is the same as *z*, then *x* is the same as *z* (transitivity), and if *x* is the same as *y*, *y* is

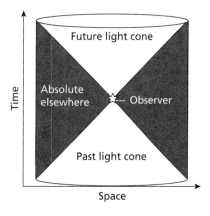

Figure 5.2 Past and future light cones

the same as x (symmetry). So if I am the same height as John, and John is the same height as Jeremy, by transitivity I am the same height as Jeremy, and by symmetry John is the same height as me. But in relativistic physics, we have no way of establishing what's at the same time as something that would allow 'the same time as' to be transitive and symmetric. Or rather, we have no *frame-invariant* way to establish what's at the same time as something that has those properties. If we had a special inertial frame that we knew was the right one to use, (e.g. because it was at absolute rest) that would be fine, we could just use that. But we have no way of settling on one special inertial frame; any choice we might make just seems really arbitrary in a way physics isn't supposed to be arbitrary. So, in relativistic physics, we accept that what is the same time as what in one inertial frame is different to another, and neither answer is better than the other, they just (literally) represent different points of view. This isn't necessarily a problem, but we have to remember that if we go from x to y using inertial frame and from y to x using another, we'll get a different value of x than what we started with.

It's still useful to be able to talk about two things being at the same time as each other. So when we do that, in physics, we always do it relative to an inertial frame. How are we to work out what's at the same time as us? Well, we imagine sending a signal that gets reflected back. We time how long it takes from when we send the signal to get the signal reflected back. If it's the same distance there and back (because we're not getting closer or further away from the thing doing the reflecting) we can just halve the time it takes to send and receive the signal, and say that halfway point is 'when the signal was reflected'. We can call this *Reichenbachian simultaneity* after Hans Reichenbach. (See Figure 5.3.)

Sending a signal and waiting for it to be reflected back was just a thought experiment, of course; we don't actually need to do that procedure every time we want to say what is the same time as what. But that thought experiment tells how to make such claims physically meaningful. Crucially, that thought experiment won't always give us the same answer for two people in the same place. When one is moving (quite fast) relative to the other, the method we've just described will give different results. That's because although the speed of light is frame-invariant (as the Michelson–Morley experiment showed) how we separate the journey into distances and

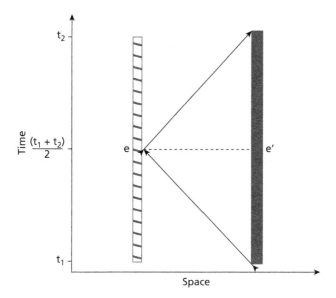

Figure 5.3 Reichenbachean simultaneity

duration will be different for the different inertial frames. A journey of a beam of light with constant speed may be shorter but take longer on one inertial frame and longer but get completed quicker on another.

The way we have been thinking of space and time has to be changed from our earlier picture. It's not just that we're now thinking of space and time as all part of the same four-dimensional structure: space–time. It's also that we are no longer thinking of this structure as Euclidean. We have a new geometry to deal with: Minkowski space–time. We can keep the same topology, and the same affine structure, but we don't get to keep the Euclidean metric. We can't rotate shapes with a guarantee that we're preserving the angles and distances involved. If we stick with a local inertial frame, we can treat that as Euclidean, and still use all that useful Newtonian metric stuff to build bridges and shoot each other, but it's not going to apply universally.

In Minkowski space–time, the space–time interval between any two events is frame-invariant. So you might disagree with an observer moving relative to you about what is at the same time as what, but you can agree about the distance in space–time. You might disagree about how long something is, but you will agree about how much space–time it takes up. Effectively, different points of view turn intervals of space–time into distances and durations in different ways.

So far, we've only been considering *Special Relativity*. That's just a special case of relativity, as the name suggests. It's the special case where we're not worried about the effects of gravity. Once we bring gravity in, we're dealing with *General* Relativity, which we briefly mentioned in chapter 2. Why bring gravity in? It turns out that *gravity changes the shape* of space–time. That is, anything with a shape, gravity changes the shape of that shape! Anything that lasts a certain amount of time, gravity changes the duration of that time! You can't understand space and time without also having an account of gravity. A weighty subject indeed...

So far, we've been imagining an inertial frame to be like Galileo's ship – the room in which nothing is moving relative to anything else, where it may or may not be moving, but no acceleration is going on. But in General Relativity, there's a sense in which that room *is* accelerating; upwards. We left you lying on the bed in the room feeling your weight pressing against the mattress. In General Relativity this is explained by the bed accelerating upwards at 9.81m/s^2. Rather than your weight pressing down on the mattress, we could say that the mattress is pressing up on you, stopping you falling downwards.

In General Relativity, freefall is counted as the basic inertial frame. If you are floating in outer space, beyond the gravitational influence (somehow) of stars and planets, that's going to count as an inertial frame. But when you come into the path of a massive object (i.e. one with lots of mass) you will get drawn towards it. You might, as Newton did, think of this as a force pulling you towards the planet/star/whatever. But in General Relativity, we think of this as being a *curved* space–time, where you are just carrying along without external forces acting upon you. You're still in an inertial frame. *Not* heading towards the centre of gravity is the thing that needs explaining, and involves some force constantly pushing you away, like the bed pushing up against your body.

General Relativity is particularly important around blackholes, which are the most massive things we know about. But it's also important because it means light (which by definition always travels in straight lines) will be affected by gravity. It's not so much that gravity will bend the beam of light – I've just said that it always travels in straight lines – it's that *what counts as straight* will change.

This sounds like some crazy theory that some guy who looks like Einstein came up with. In a sense it is. It's a theory, Einstein came up with it, and it's crazy. But it's also one of the *best confirmed scientific theories* we have.

THE TWINS PARADOX

When calculating distances, we can transform one path through space–time into another, by treating one path as travelling further in space in a shorter amount of time, or as travelling less far in space in a longer amount of time, depending on whose point of view we are taking up. This gives rise to what is known as 'the twins paradox'. Two twins starting and ending in the same point in space–time end up with different ages. But there is no paradox. It just requires we understand what it means to treat space and time as all part of space–time.

Let's start with a trick question: What do clocks measure? Time? No! We have subsumed space and time (and gravity) into the same space–time structure. We have no way of separating time out from that structure that is frame-invariant. In Minkowski space–time what clocks measure is the amount of space–time something travels through. Tim Maudlin uses an analogy with odometers on cars.[4] Odometers measure the distance travelled by a car, and clocks measure the distance travelled though space–time.

Two 'accurate' clocks side by side will measure the same amount of space–time, just as two cars travelling together will measure the same distance. But if one car takes a different route to the other, they may well measure a different number of miles when they arrive at the same destination. This is because you can start at the same place and finish at the same place, but nonetheless have travelled different distances.

In the so-called 'twins paradox', we imagine two twins who start in the same place and are the same age.[5] One of them is an astronaut and the other is not. Let's call them 'Astro' and 'Not', respectively. Astro gets into a rocket and travels to Mars and back. 'Not' stays at

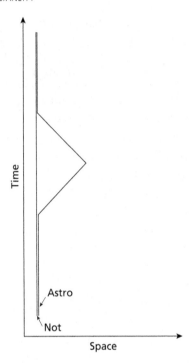

Figure 5.4 Two journeys through space-time

home.[6] Each has a very sensitive clock with them. They synchro-
nise their clocks before they set of, and then compare them on their
next meeting. Astro's clock has recorded less time as having passed
than Not's. So, despite being twins, Astro is now *younger* than Not.
(See Figure 5.4.)

Given the way I set it up, you may have been expecting Not to
be younger; after all, Astro has done all the travelling! But in fact,
Not's clock measures the bigger amount of space–time. This is a
feature of the geometry of space–time. Remember, we can't expect
to conduct transformations preserving distances and durations in
this geometry.

From Not's point of view, Astro's journey away and his journey back take the same length of time, as depicted in Figure 5.4.
Astro's clock seems to tick at a faster rate on the way out, and a
slower rate on the way back, and he will come back having aged

less than Not. From Astro's point of view, Not will appear to have slowed down his rate of aging as Astro moves away from Not, and to have sped it up on the return journey. See Figure 5.5. But if Not appears to age at half the rate on the way out, and at twice the rate on the way back, you would expect things to even out. This doesn't happen because, from Astro's perspective, the journey out takes longer than the journey back. The point at which Astro appears to start the return journey to Not is labelled with a +. What Not looks like to Astro at the start of Astro's return journey is marked with a small ★. Look at what happens when Astro changes direction halfway through. From Astro's point of view this is instantaneous, but Not's clock appears to have jumped significantly during the change. This jump is where the 'extra' time on Not's clock comes in.

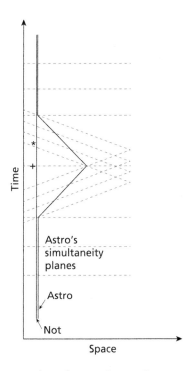

Figure 5.5 Two journeys through space-time, again

PUTNAM'S PROBLEM

Hilary Putnam is most widely associated with the argument that relativistic physics rules out the passage of time.[7] We'll review his argument, and show that rejecting an absolute present isn't quite the same as rejecting McTchange. A defender of a dynamic view does have a difficult decision to make about how it responds to this argument though.

Putnam considers three assumptions, and draws out a tension from them:

1. The moment at which you are currently located is real.
2. At least one other observer is real, and it is possible for this other observer to be in motion relative to you.
3. There are no privileged observers.

The assumption that there are no privileged observers amounts to a claim that if one observer-at-a-time is real, and stands in the right kind of relation to another, the other observer must also be real. That is, we can't pick out a particular observer who is special, or lives in the inertial-frame which is objectively not moving. The other observer moving relative to you has an equal claim to be real that doesn't depend on you. This 'right kind of relation' that you and the other observer are in, Putnam goes on to say, must be a physical relation that is independent of the choice of a coordinate system and can be defined in terms of the fundamental notions of physics.

The idea is that because of relativity, the sorts of relations that will count as being 'of the right kind' will mean that the past and future must be real.

Remember our twins in the previous section, Astro and Not. As Figure 5.5 shows, they disagree about what's simultaneous.

From Not's point of view, what is simultaneous is just given by horizontal comparison of positions, but not according to Astro. What's simultaneous from Astro's point of view follows this sequence:

1. What's simultaneous is horizontal, just as for Not.
2. When Astro accelerates the simultaneity plane slopes down towards Not until the return journey begins.
3. For the return journey the simultaneity planes slope up until Astro arrives.
4. On arrival the simultaneity planes become horizontal again.

Being at the same time as something is normally thought to be an example of a transitive and symmetric relation, as explained above. If it entails the existence of both things related by it, if you exist, any observer at the same time as you exists, and any observer at the same time as *them* exists. But what's at the same time as them, relative to *their* inertial frame, differs from what's at the same time as them relative to *your* inertial frame. If both 'same time as' relations are existence entailing, both locations in space–time have an equal claim to exist. Since neither of you are privileged, we can't claim one of the 'same time as' relations is existence entailing and the other isn't.

To return to Astro and Not, we are going to go from Not at the bit labelled + to Astro, and from Astro (now using Astro's inertial frame) to Not at the bit labelled ★. So both the location + and the location ★ are equally real.

'Entailment' here is just the term for something being a logical consequence of something else. An existence entailing relation, then, is a relation that can only relate existing things. So if an existence entailing relation relates two or more things, it's a logical consequence that they all exist. I can imagine things that don't exist; imagining isn't an existence entailing relation. Heating something looks like it is existence entailing; if one thing heats another, they must both exist.

What's happened here should be clear. If we treat a relative definition of simultaneity as if it's existence entailing, but take existence to be an absolute matter, we end up claiming past and future times exist. This is because *relative to some other inertial frames* past and future times are at the same time as points in space–time that are (relative to your inertial frame) at the same time as you. The lesson is equally clear. Either existence is not absolute, or relative simultaneity doesn't require both observers-at-times to exist.

It might be tempting to draw a further lesson from this: change is mere temporal variation, and there is no McTchange. The temptation comes from this line of thought: McTchange is change in what is present. If the Universe doesn't provide an absolute global sequence of successive present times (a 'foliation'), then it can't change what time is present. We should not draw that conclusion from Putnam's argument, however.

The link between McTchange and an absolute global succession of presents hasn't been argued for yet. If there were such a succession, it would require McTchange, but it has not been established that we can only have McTchange if we have a unique foliation of the Universe.

Defenders of McTchange do have to face a dilemma, however. Do they claim that there is some privileged inertial frame (perhaps undiscovered, perhaps unknowable) that provides such an absolute global succession of present times, or do they claim that McTchange is real, but that there is not a global present?

The evidence for McTchange, as we have seen, seems to come from our first-personal awareness of persisting through time (by contrast to spreading out over space). This evidence simply doesn't say anything about what is at the same time as what in the Universe. But it is troubling to think that the question 'what is happening on Mars now?' might not have a physically meaningful answer, besides a claim about how Mars appears from our perspective.

QUANTUM GRAVITY

As we saw in chapter 2, Quantum Gravity is an attempt to reconcile General Relativity, and Quantum Mechanics. If Putnam's argument is supposed to show that relativistic physics is a reason for rejecting McTchange, it really matters what, if any, role there is for time on the theory that supersedes relativity. If we somehow get a foliation of the Universe from Quantum Gravity, that means that we can claim that McTchange is compatible with an absolute global succession of presents after all. But if that's what you want, the news doesn't look good.

There are a number of competing views of Quantum Gravity. *String Theory* is perhaps the best known, but *Loop Quantum Gravity*, *Canonical Quantum Gravity*, *Causal Set Theory* and others also have prominent defenders.[8] For these views, getting something like the relativistic space–time we have been discussing above is a challenge. That's because the fundamental level of reality according to these views looks quite different from what we have discussed so far.

String Theory, as the name suggests, is the theory that the Universe is made up of (incredibly small) 'strings'. These strings vibrate in up to eleven dimensions. That's more than the four we were used to in space–time. While there are ways to get four-dimensional space–time out of String Theory, it seems to be open to a range of interpretations, and justifying the four-dimensional one as the correct interpretation of the theory remains a challenge.

The other theories don't start with an eleven-dimensional structure that we then attempt to extract four-dimensional space–time from. They start with a basic structure, such as a 'spin foam', a 'causal set', or something, that we then attempt to show relativistic space–time as emerging from at the scales and energy levels at which we normally observe the world.

It is very much a live question whether McTchange is possible on whatever view Quantum Gravity delivers. Lee Smolin, a defender of Loop Quantum Gravity, argues that we must understand the Universe (and even the laws of nature) as evolving in time, whereas Carlo Rovelli, also a defender of Loop Quantum Gravity, argues that the view shows time is not fundamental to physics. Julian Barbour argues that we must adopt an approach that dispenses with time, even in the sense needed for a static view of time, whereas Fay Dowker defends a version of Causal Set Theory in which she explicitly defends the passage of time, and gives an account of it as the birth of space–time atoms.

These theories are highly technical, and, frankly, I don't understand them. Indeed, the details of these theories are live research topics in theoretical physics. Even if one can get the maths to work, generating empirical predictions that allows physicists to test these theories remains a challenge. And even if we can establish which theory is correct, working out how to turn the maths into claims about what reality is like remains a *further* challenge. There is no shortage of challenges! But even on the most optimistic reading for a defender of McTchange, we're not going to get anything like the Newtonian picture of absolute space and time back.

On many of the views, time is simply not part of the fundamental picture of reality, and the structure of space–time arises only at certain scales, or is projected by humans onto the world. And on those views where time is claimed to pass, we don't get a global succession of presents. Take Causal Set Theory as an example. This gives us some things that are causally upstream of other things, and some things that are causally downstream. It also allows that lots of things are not causally related to each other. So two things (B and C) might both be causally downstream of A and upstream of D, but neither downstream or upstream of each other.

There's room for McTchange in these causal sequences. Time flows from the earlier, causally upstream events, to the later causally downstream events. So there's McTchange from A being present to B being present, to D being present (or alternatively from A to C to D). But there's a puzzle about B and C. B and C are neither earlier, nor later, *nor at the same time as each other* on these views, because time comes from the causal structure and they are not causally ordered with respect to each other. Some philosophers worry that the 'causal structure' that allows this isn't that similar to the way we previously thought about time and causation.[9]

At the start of this chapter, we considered the view that physics had shown that Relativity caused a problem for McTchange. It's not the case that our best physics rules McTchange out. In fact, the existence of McTchange is a matter of live debate amongst physicists. But the idea of an absolute, global succession of presents either involves a means of foliating the Universe we haven't discovered, one that cannot be made physically meaningful, or the prospect of foliating the Universe in a unique way needs to be given up.

We have scratched the surface of some very difficult issues; ones that involve complex mathematics, technical and abstract ideas, and areas where the understanding of the issues is still hazy even for the experts. This book is intended as a basic introduction to the philosophy of time. I want to finish the chapter by addressing two questions: 'Why bother including this material?' and 'Why bother including any other material?'.

The first question can be answered by pointing out what the chapter has shown; that there is a relationship between the actual physics in the world and the phenomena to be explained in philosophy of time. It is important to acknowledge that the philosophical questions should be informed by our best physical theories. The second question is provoked by the thought that the philosophical questions should be left to the physicists; that there is no contribution left for the untechnical thinker in their armchair. Ideally, the armchair philosophers should only sit in their respective armchairs after becoming reasonably well informed about the world beyond their study. But the sorts of issues that philosophy is concerned with go beyond those issues that physics is concerned with. Indeed, the very question of what topics are the proper concern of the physicist is a philosophical question. The questions discussed in this chapter and the next (which also concerns topics in physics) are intimately linked to other topics in the philosophy of time that are more obviously distant from the concerns of physicists. We will be discussing many of those topics throughout this book. For a philosopher of time, the issues flow into one another without a clear demarcation between issues for physicists, classicists, historians, economists or ethicists. Where the concerns of physicists and philosophers overlap, we must rely on the work of specialist philosophers of physics who can understand the issues both as scientific theory and philosophical speculation.

QUESTIONS FOR DISCUSSION

1. If we can't get physical evidence of absolute rest, should we abandon a commitment to there being an inertial frame at absolute rest?
2. Why would it be useful to have a frame-invariant metric for space–time?
3. What response should a defender of a dynamic view make to Putnam's argument?

NOTES

1 Or, as Baron, Miller and Tallant (2022) suggest, even less! Maybe they don't need time at all.
2 It being one dimensional, it doesn't make sense for time to have an affine structure. And we can only have a metrical structure for time if there are things that happen with a constant repeated pattern that we can say happen the same amount of time apart.
3 And so to create more and more accurate means of killing people from a long way away. Hooray for progress!
4 Maudlin (2012:76)
5 It's very rare that twins are *exactly* the same age, because giving birth is not instantaneous, and tends to happen a baby at a time. But ignore this.
6 So we don't feel to sorry for Not, imagine that they are holding lots of parties.
7 Putnam (1967)
8 For String Theory see Kane (2017); for Loop Quantum Gravity see Smolin (2009) and Rovelli and Vidotto (2015). For Canonical Quantum Gravity see Barbour (1999); for Causal Set Theory see Dowker (2014).
9 Baron Miller and Tallant (2022: chapter 5)

FURTHER READING

For comparatively non-technical introductions to Relativistic Physics:

Maudlin (2012) *and* Sklar (1977) are accessible and informative.

On Putnam's problem, see Putnam (1967); the original paper is quite readable and non-technical.

On the idea that we get rid of time from physics see Baron, Miller, and Tallant (2022).

THE ARROW OF TIME

Besides the question of whether change is best characterised as McTchange or as mere temporal variation, there are other questions we might have about the nature of time. The 'arrow' of time refers to the directedness of time. Even if we thought that being past and being future are to be understood in terms of being earlier than some subjective point in time, or being later than it, we might still think that the earlier and later directions are objectively different.

In this chapter, we will be focussed on the arrow of time. As we shall see, there are lots of respects in which the past appears different to the future. One of the challenges will be thinking about how these differences relate to each other. Is there one difference that forms the basis for the others? If there is, which is it?

THE ASYMMETRIES OF TIME

THE ASYMMETRY OF RECORDS

Let's think for a bit about what makes the past seem different to the future. One of the first things that you might notice is that we can remember the past and not the future. Memory isn't the only way we know things about other times. We can know quite a lot about what's going to happen; we are very good at predicting the future (especially in controlled environments like laboratories). Given an understanding of the rules by which a system changes, and the current state of the system, we can predict what's going to happen. If the rules only leave one option open, we can predict what that will

DOI: 10.4324/9781003189459-6

be, and if they leave multiple options, we can often predict how likely those options will be. Prediction is *really useful*.

Not all systems can be predicted, however. Uncertainty limits the precision of predictions. We might not know the rules by which a system evolves. Our ability to measure the present state of the relevant system also limits our ability to predict how it evolves. *Chaotic systems* are those where small changes to the conditions of a system make a large difference to how it evolves. The weather system is a classic case of a chaotic system. Although the rules by which air currents move are well understood, very small changes in air currents can produce a large change in weather a while later. In fact, it's unlikely we'll ever be in a position to measure all of the relevant states of the global weather system accurately enough to predict it with certainty. *Stochastic systems*, by contrast, are ones where the rules for the evolution of the system are chancy; that is the way the system evolves is a matter of probability rather than determinacy. There will be uncertainty in predicting both chaotic and stochastic systems, but for stochastic systems, the chanciness of the laws by which the system evolves are the source of the uncertainty, rather than an inability to measure the state of the system precisely enough. 'Prediction' tends to be reserved for the future; the equivalent for the past isn't memory, but 'retrodiction'. Retrodiction works the same as prediction, except we 'evolve' the system in a different direction.

We can predict the future, and retrodict the past (subject to worries about chaotic and stochastic systems). But we can also remember the past, and we can't remember the future. Or at least, some people claim to have 'premonitions' which are the future counterpart of memories, but if there are genuine premonitions, they are much, much less common than memories. This needs explanation.

So far, this could be a quirk of human psychology, but we can formulate this asymmetry in purely physical terms. We have *records* of the past, but no equivalent records of the future. Consider a few examples of analogue records, for a moment. The rings exposed in the trunk of a felled tree record how old the tree is; the light rings record periods of fast growth in the spring and early summer, and the dark rings record periods of slower growth in late summer and autumn. The width of the tree rings records how good the climate was for growing. And trees are just a particularly nice example. We are able to infer much about what the past was like because we have records that, if we know how to interpret them, allow us to make those inferences. We can find out things about the past that we couldn't know by retrodiction, because we can interpret records of the past. We have no equivalent records of the future. Memory is just a (not always reliable) special case of a record of the past. So we can call this asymmetry **the asymmetry of records**. Any good account of the arrow of time will have to account for the asymmetry of records.

THE ASYMMETRY OF INTERVENTION

It's not just our ability to make inferences about the past that makes it different from the future. It seems like we can intervene on the future in a way that we can't intervene on the past. So, if my bathroom is flooded, I can do things to make it dry out quicker, but I can't do things to make it not have flooded. When you conduct an experiment, you intervene on a system to see how it evolves, but the intervention seems to have its effects *after* your intervention rather than before. Maybe you think that there are some exceptions, but it is definitely much, much more common for effects to come after their causes than before.[1]

There are lots of situations where we can't intervene on the future or the past. Sometimes we simply lack 'causal handles' (i.e. means by which to affect things). Sometimes we are too far away to do anything in time, or don't have any options that change the result. King Cnut of England (1016–1035) is reported to have had his chair placed on the foreshore and to have commanded the tide not to come in. This intervention was ineffective.[2] Cnut, it seems, was rather theatrically making a point that sometimes even kings cannot intervene. The asymmetry of intervention, then, is not that we can *never* intervene on the past where we can *always* intervene on the future, but that while we can sometimes intervene on the future, we can never intervene on the past.

It might seem as though we *can* in fact intervene on the past. We can of course change how the past relates to present or future things. If a court passes a judgement, and the appeals court overturns it, it looks like the past has been changed. It used to be the case that the judgement was law, and now it is the case that it never was. This is because what is the law depends on present and future facts about how the legal system will treat something. So, there's a sense in which we can change the past by changing the status of some past event in relation to the present and future. This sort of case will be the topic of chapter 9.

When we discuss the asymmetry of intervention, we are thinking of intervening on the 'intrinsic' state of some system, i.e. the way it is independent of other systems. Where we are considering a wholly past system, we cannot intervene on its intrinsic state. If we are understanding intervention in this way, you might think that we can't intervene on future systems either. If we specify that the system is wholly future, to the extent that it makes sense to talk of a future system at all, it's far too early to intervene. But we can do things presently, that will affect the intrinsic conditions of future systems in a way that we cannot do for past systems.

THE ASYMMETRY OF REFERENCE

It seems like our ability to talk about the past is different from our ability to talk about future things. I can describe a set of circumstances equally well whether the supposed circumstances are past or future. To that extent, talking about the future is easy. But it seems like I can talk directly about past things in a way that I cannot about future things. I can recall my late grandfather, and talk about *that* man, in a way that I can't talk about my grandchildren. I have no grandchildren to speak of.

It's not just that I don't know whether I will have grandchildren. We can come up with a description of a future set of circumstances that we know will occur. But if it describes an individual, and that individual doesn't exist yet, we simply can't refer directly to that person in the way we can to people we've met.[3] We can't 'have them in mind' or think *of* them, rather than merely thinking about the content of a description. This is what I'm calling the *asymmetry of reference*.

THE ASYMMETRY OF AFFECT

We seem to have different attitudes towards past and future. We hope for good things in the future, but it doesn't quite make sense to hope for things in the past. Similarly, we can be nostalgic for a past time, but it doesn't seem to make sense to have nostalgia for a future time. Regret seems to be past-directed, as does relief.

It might be that these words just have directedness as part of their meaning (the way 'prediction' is for the future, and 'retrodiction' is for the past). But it seems plausible, I think, that the connection between regret and pastness goes a bit deeper than a convention about how we use the term. There's something about past actions that makes regret understandable, where there's something odd about regretting what we're going to do. If you think you are going to regret what you're going to do, it seems like you should *not do it*. Or if you can't avoid doing it, don't regret it; there was nothing you could do, after all. We can think of cases where you know that you will not entirely be in control of your actions, where it might make sense to regret your future actions, and we can distinguish between regret and remorse, where regret is sadness that a bad thing happened and remorse involves treating oneself as responsible. But it looks like *bad faith* to anticipate that you are going to do something:

- for which you are responsible
- that you think will rightly be a cause for remorse,
- and not to attempt preventing that outcome.

It's tempting to say either you are not really responsible, or you should prevent the outcome.

It looks like we need to account for these sorts of differences of attitude between past and future. Let's call these differences the *asymmetry of affect*.

TIME'S ARROW: ENTROPY VERSUS CAUSATION

The asymmetries of affect and reference are pretty noticeable, but it seems like they can be explained in terms of the asymmetries of records and intervention. In order to refer directly to something in the relevant sense, we need to have had causal contact of some kind. This could be direct, or it could be indirect. I have never met my great-grandfather, though my father (who I have met) has, and I have held some objects that used to belong to my great-grandfather that plausibly contain records of his existence. If I were to look at a photograph of him, for example, that would plausibly allow me to refer to him in the relevant way. It looks like I lack the relevant causal contact with the future; I have no records of it, where I have records of my great-grandfather, in the form of his possessions, a photograph of him, and the memories of my father.

The various different emotional attitudes can, I suspect, be explained by uncertainty about the future, my ability to intervene on later events, but not earlier ones, and my awareness, through my own memory, of the past, that makes me aware of a continuing narrative of my own life (we'll come back to this in chapter 10).

The central question for the rest of this chapter, then, is whether we think the asymmetry of records and the asymmetry of intervention are accounted for by *the entropic gradient* or by *causation*. I'll hold off for now explaining what entropy means, and simply say that the entropic gradient is an increasing level of disorder in the universe. Causation is what *makes* a system evolve from one state to the next.[4] Both are candidate explanations for the arrow of time, and there is wide agreement that both causation (in *some* form) and the entropic gradient are features of the universe. The question is whether we look to the entropic gradient to explain causation, or whether we look to causation to explain the entropic gradient.

TIME-REVERSAL INVARIANCE

Before we move on to causation versus entropy, let's observe one of the things that makes the arrow of time such an interesting topic. We have so far discussed four (groups of) asymmetries we might notice between past and future. That the future differs from the past seems so obvious that only a philosopher would question it.[5] But the laws of physics all seem to be ones that work the same in both directions. That's why we can retrodict just as well as we can predict. If you use the laws of physics, and you want to know how a system will evolve, the laws are exactly the same regardless of which direction you go in. The technical term for this is that they are *time-reversal invariant*.

It's really obvious that the past is different from the future. But how can something so obvious *not show up* in the laws of physics? Especially since the ability to conduct physics experiments and remember the results depends on the asymmetries of intervention and of records! Physics makes *use* of the asymmetries that don't show up in its laws. The challenge for an account of the arrow of time, then, is to explain how we end up with these asymmetries given that the laws of nature are time-reversal invariant.

ASIDE ON STATISTICAL MECHANICS

Imagine you want to know what a physical system is going to do. One option is to know the exact location and velocity of every particle, and then to calculate what each particle will do, including all the interactions with the other particles. This is rather impractical. Another option is to come up with some generalisations about what physical systems with particular features do, and then make a claim that very probably the physical system will obey that generalisation. It's these generalisations that will allow us to find an asymmetry in nature.

The temperature of an object is equivalent to the average kinetic energy of the particles that compose that object – that is, how much the average particle moves around. We don't need to know the position of each of these particles and their velocities to know that if you place a hot object somewhere colder, some of the energy from the hot object will transfer to the cold surroundings. The hot object will cool down, and the cold surroundings will warm up. Statistical mechanics can show this by showing that there are lots of different combinations of position and velocity that result in particles with lots of kinetic energy transferring energy to particles with less kinetic energy, and comparatively few combinations of position and velocity that transfer energy in the other direction. Statistical mechanics can show us why hot things heat cool things, and cool things cool hot things.

The study of the transfer of heat is *thermodynamics*. But since heat is mean kinetic energy, discoveries from thermodynamics are in fact much more general. They apply to transfers of energy generally. And since you can't transfer *information* without transferring energy (because something has to carry the information), thermodynamics also tells us about transferring information.

Temperature is the kind of property we find in the world around us, at the sort of medium-sized 'macroscopic' scale at which we live. The kinetic energy of a particle is a property that we find at microscopic scales that we need specialist equipment to observe.

Statistical mechanics is useful for taking us from microscopic properties to macroscopic properties, using probabilities. And thermodynamics makes use of statistical mechanics to tell us things about how medium-sized objects are *almost certain* to behave.

ENTROPY

One key concept we will need in what follows is that of **entropy**. Entropy is a measure of the 'disorder' or 'mixed-upness' of a system. In fact, it is a measure of the number of ways a state can be achieved in a system. Suppose I have all my books sorted into colour order, from red, via orange, yellow, green and blue, to purple. Perhaps a few pairs of books are the same colour and could go in either order, but nonetheless there are very few orderings that are going to count as being my books in colour order from red to purple. Were my books arranged that way, that would have low entropy (i.e. low 'disorder') because there are few ways of putting them in that state. Now consider the case where my books are *not* in colour order. There are *loads* of ways of them not being in colour order. Arranging them alphabetically, or by height, or grouping them by topic, or when I got them, would all do that. But so, probably, would just arranging them randomly. Arranging them alphabetically, or by height, or by topic, or when I bought them would all be low entropy states, because for each of them there are very few ways of arranging them that would count as being in that state. But arranging them in some way that was none of those orders could be achieved really easily. I could do it by moving almost any book!

Let's just link this into temperature, to see how it applies. If all the fast-moving particles are next to each other, that's low entropy, because there are relatively few ways of achieving that. If they are evenly spread out throughout the system, there are lots of ways of mixing particles up to achieve that, so that's high entropy. So a system where the heat is in one place has lower entropy than the same system (with the same overall temperature), where the heat is evenly spread out.

We notice that very frequently hot things cool down, but very rarely do cold things warm up (without transferring energy from somewhere else). And statistical mechanics explains that this is because it is vastly more likely for heat to spread out than to collect in one place. In fact, we can treat this as a law of nature. Entropy in a closed system will increase. Entropy will only decrease in a system if energy is transferred from outside the system, but if we consider the larger system that includes the energy source, the entropy of *that* system will increase. So, making your fridge cooler than the room around it is lowering the entropy, but it does so by using energy to pump out heat. The system is not closed, though, and the entropy of the whole system, including the power station and the rest of your kitchen, increases. You have won the battle against entropy in a small cupboard, but you cannot win the war. It ends in the 'heat death of the universe' where energy is spread out around the universe as evenly as it will go.[6]

The claim that entropy of a closed system increases is a rough statement of the *2nd Law of Thermodynamics*. This is nearly, but not quite, the exception to the time-reversal invariance of the laws of nature. Frustratingly, this law too is time-reversal invariant. We haven't yet said anything about which direction entropy will increase in! We just know that it will go from low to high. It could be, for all that the 2nd Law says, that *this* moment, *right now*, is the lowest entropy one, and that past and future both see increases in entropy as we move away from the present. We need something extra to get a temporal asymmetry of entropy. We need either the start of the universe or the end to have the lowest entropy.

Spoiler: it's the start.

THE PAST HYPOTHESIS

Suppose the past were very low entropy. That would explain a lot. Because not only does statistical mechanics tell us that entropy will rise in a closed system, but we notice that entropy rises. We notice that it is more common for ripples to radiate out from stones dropped in water, rather than ripples radiating in and expelling stones from water. We see ice-cubes melt into cold puddles, but not cold puddles rise up to form solid cube shapes.[7]

If we *suppose* that the past was the lowest entropy the universe ever gets, and then have the 2nd Law of Thermodynamics tell us that entropy increases, we have an asymmetry between past and future.

The past is low entropy and the future is high entropy. There is an increase in entropy over time that we can call *the entropic gradient*.

If we return to our asymmetry of records, we can make sense of why we can remember the past and not the future, because the entropic gradient allows us to work out how things must have been earlier. We can find out about both the past and future by making inferences from the laws of nature and how things are now, but armed with the past hypothesis, we can go beyond retrodiction to understand how the past was. This is because we know that certain bits of the universe, when acted upon, change in predictable ways. If we see a fossil, we can best explain the marks in the rock by thinking about how the sediment that became rock was changed by the presence of the plant or animal that got fossilised. It's not, as Albert (2000:117) points out, that we can simply retrodict from the fossil we have now, to the existence of an animal in the distant past. We instead can take the state the sediment *very probably* would have been in before an animal was there, and the state it is in now, and infer that some change happened in between. So it's not an inference from now to an earlier time, but an inference from two times, before and after some change, to a time in the middle. The past hypothesis is what allows us to infer that it's much more likely that there was a lower entropy before condition that resulted in this highly unusual after condition, because the (highly organised) patterns in the rock are much more likely to result from a change that happened to the sediment than they are to have arisen by chance.

It's *possible*, of course, that what we *think* is a record is just a chance arrangement of things that looks like a record. It's physically possible that particles in the universe could spontaneously get arranged so as to be exactly like the brain of a person experiencing reading a book. *Incredibly* unlikely, but *possible*. Much more likely is that your apparent memory of reading the previous sentence is a result of the alteration of your brain by reading the sentence.

We have, so far, only *supposed* that the past was low entropy. As a supposition, it is very satisfying. Were it true we could explain the asymmetry of records, and also the asymmetry of intervention. The entropic gradient is such that the higher entropy end of a change allows for more arrangements than the lower entropy end. There are more options for a higher entropy end of a change. So if we accept that entropy increases over time, it makes sense that we would see the rippling out of multiple effects following from a single cause.

There's something deeply unsatisfying about this, of course. It's not usually considered good science to suppose something because it would be much more convenient if it were true.[8] But there's not a test that we could do to check. Any test we could do of the world presently available to us won't tell the difference between a world in which there are records and one in which there aren't but it happens to look as if there are. All we have immediate access to is how things are now. Only if we are allowed to believe in a before state that would change to create a record, can we test claims about the past. And we can only believe in that if we accept the past hypothesis.

The past hypothesis seems important to explain the asymmetry of records, which is pretty fundamental to our explaining any experience we have of the world. But our explanation so far of why we should accept the past hypothesis is just that it is needed to explain why memories and records allow us to remember things/find out things about the past.

No-one serious doubts that there is an entropic gradient, nor that this plays an important role in explaining why the past seems different to the future. But there's an extra step or two open to you at this point. You could say that the arrow of time *is* the entropic gradient. If, in a small corner of space-time, the improbable but possible local reversal of the entropic gradient occurs, time would reverse too, in that local area. But you could instead say that the arrow of time *explains* the entropic gradient. We will consider this in the next section. Or, we could say that there is no arrow of time, but that we confuse the entropic gradient for a direction of time. We will discuss that after we've dealt with causation.

CAUSATION

The entropic gradient isn't the only game in town for explaining the asymmetries of records and intervention. It might be that there is something else that explains those asymmetries *and* the entropic gradient. It might be that causation brings about changes, and it is a feature of causation that the entropy of effects is higher than the entropy of causes. That means we take the story we had before about entropy explaining the arrow of time, but say that the arrow of time is the arrow of causation.

Fitting causation into our story can go in various ways. Here are some features of the story I particularly like. Each bit of the universe brings the next bit into existence through a causal process. We have reason to believe in causation because of our awareness of our ability to intervene on the world. Our awareness of our own ability to intervene on the world isn't merely because there are more arrangements on the high entropy side of a change, but because we *bring about* changes. If our experience of intervening on the world is an experience of making things happen, producing effects and bringing about consequences, we can stretch this experience of us causing things to an understanding of one event causing another without our involvement.[9] So I can use my understanding of creating waves in the bathtub to understand why Cnut was unable to hold back the tide by royal decree.

There are different ways we might think about causation. The 'best-systems' view says that the universe is just an arrangement of local particular matters of fact related in various scientifically describable ways. Talk of causation, on this view, is just a way of summarising those sequences of matters of fact that represent regularities. We might want to distinguish the causal regularities from the coincidental ones, so we might say that we are focussed on the ones where we can say 'if that cause hadn't have happened, the effect wouldn't have'. But on this 'best systems' view, we're just summarising the sequence of states of the world in a particularly efficient way that allows us to make predictions and retrodictions.[10]

Causation can be given more *oomph* however. You can have a view of causation in which it doesn't merely allow summaries and inferences, but it *makes* things happen, *brings things about, produces effects*. It governs what happens, rather than merely summarises. On this view of causation, the universe unfolds in the way it does, because causation makes it do that. Effects never come before their causes. Our awareness of intervening on the world (from getting out of bed, to conducting experiments) is our awareness of making things happen.

I confess, I think causation has to involve making things happen, rather than merely describing patterns. But whenever I try to explain what this making, or producing, or bringing about *is* it's difficult to do so. I quickly find myself doing an impression of someone cheering on a faltering marathon runner. GIVE IT SOME OOMPH! MAKE IT HAPPEN! Much like a tiring marathon runner, it is open for defenders of the summarising view to say that they are giving it all the oomph there is to give. The defenders of the summarising view will say that this is what making things happen looks like: first one thing and then another, where the second wouldn't be there without the first.

Suppose that you go for a view of causation where the direction of causation gives the arrow of time. You still have some choices to make. You could defend a *causal theory* of time. This is a view where you turn explanations about what time is into explanations about what causation is. It has the advantage that you need to explain fewer things in your theory. Buy one account of causation, get an account of time for free! It has a significant disadvantage, though, which is that it doesn't work. The chief objection to the causal theory of time is that it starts to look like our grasp on causation is itself tied to an understanding of what time is. On the one hand we can't understand intervention unless we know what change is. An intervention is a type of change after all! But also, there are issues in deciding which direction is before and which after on the basis of causation. In trying to use causation we seem to rely on this distinction to establish what is a candidate cause for what. My own preference is to think that causation and time go together not because one can be explained in terms of the other, but because each can only be explained alongside the other.

C-THEORIES OF TIME

We have so far discussed two prominent accounts of the arrow of time: one says that the entropic gradient provides the arrow of time (and so explains the asymmetries of records, of intervention, of reference and of affect). The other says that causation gives the arrow of time (and so explains the asymmetry of intervention, the entropic gradient, the asymmetry of records, and the asymmetries of reference and affect). You could, if you were a little more radical, say that there is no arrow of time; what there is *instead* is the entropic gradient. You might claim that humans project time onto the world, because we live in a region of space-time that has a consistent entropic gradient, but we should not infer from conditions round here to conditions across the universe. Time is a bunch of local conventions, rather than a fundamental feature of nature. Not only is McTchange not real, but mere temporal variation isn't either. There's just the entropic gradient, and a bunch of (scientifically unsupported) ways of talking about it.

Both these views appeal to the entropic gradient to explain why we think there's a difference between past and future, and they disagree whether the explanation shows what in the world provides that difference, or what explains our talking as if there's one.

The view that there is no arrow to time is known as the C-theory. You may remember we discussed it in chapter 1. This view, it is important to understand, isn't a view that claims that we are systematically mistaken about the asymmetries we have been thinking about. They can accept that we really do observe all of those asymmetries *around here*. And it makes perfect sense, they can say, that creatures like us think about time the way we do; when humans evolved, paying attention to these differences would have been useful, given the evidence humans have access to. This is not a view, like Zeno's view that motion is impossible (from chapter 2), where we are meant to ignore experience in favour of logical considerations. On the contrary, this view claims we should be guided by the evidence, and not be too quick to go beyond it. We know what our experiences of time are like, but they are based on a tiny region of space-time, and are compatible with there being regions of space-time that work differently. Given how we have evolved, creatures like us are bound to think in terms of before and after, but that doesn't guarantee that the universe independently does contain a split between before and after. And if fundamental physical theories don't need an arrow of time, then we shouldn't believe in one. As we saw in the previous chapter, what our fundamental physical theories need is still up for grabs, but it is at least plausible that physicists might explain the world without there being a fundamental arrow to time.

FRAMING THE DEBATE

In chapter 1 we had a debate between two views of change. One where change was variation over time, and another where change had some (mysterious?) extra thing that made it different to space.

We find ourselves in a similar situation. Causation might just be a sequence of things that depend on what went before, or it might involve some (mysterious?) extra thing that produces the next bit of the universe. In fact, the views tend to come as packages. The view of change as temporal variation often tends to go with the view of causation as a device for summarising the universe. The view that there is McTchange tends to go with causation as involving a McTchange that shapes how the world is. But nothing about the positions forces them into packages like that, and you can hold them in any combination. You shouldn't, obviously, because three of those four combinations are wrong. But you could.

Don't look to the physicists to settle these debates for you. We're dealing here with what story we tell about the world that goes beyond what we can directly observe. We can only observe what is happening, not what could have happened but didn't. With the assumption of past hypothesis (and/or with the rule that causes always come before their effects) we can tell things about what did happen. But we can't do a physics experiment that tells us what *must* happen, only what does. We can only directly observe bits of the universe that are in our past light-cone, and that are not hidden behind the other bits. But physics is supposed to make theories that apply to the other bits too. Whichever view we are more attracted to, we are going beyond the evidence we get from physics into a choice of different hypotheses based on wider theoretical considerations. We shouldn't ignore the physics; it's really very important in getting our theories right. But it isn't going to deliver an answer about the world that isn't itself based on a load of theoretical/philosophical assumptions.

The oomphy, productive view of causation I describe above has some significant consequences. If the arrow of time is the direction of causation, that changing (the intrinsic state of) the past is ruled out by definition. There can be no 'backwards' causation. Whereas if the arrow of time *is* the entropic gradient, backwards causation will be rare, but is physically possible. So one of the differences between the two hypotheses on which there is an arow of time will be what we say about the rare circumstances in which in a local area the entropic gradient reverses. Does time reverse with it, or are there merely some unusual causal effects? We will revisit this worry about changing the past again in the next chapter.

QUESTIONS FOR DISCUSSION

1. Come up with examples of differences between the past and future. Are they examples of the asymmetries of records, intervention, reference or affect, or some other asymmetry?
2. Neither the level of entropy in the past, nor the causal connectedness of natural events can be directly observed. What count as good reasons for including them in our best theory?
3. Are we entitled to think that time works in the same way in parts of the universe we haven't observed as it does during the places and time that you have observed?

NOTES

1   We'll return to the possibility of backwards causation later in the chapter.
2   Some kind of embankment may have been more effective, as an intervention strategy. Intervention is not just a question of *whether* one intervenes, but also of *how*.
3   In philosophy of language, this is known as 'singular reference'. Some people deny that there are any cases of singular reference, in which case they won't recognise there being an asymmetry of reference. Valberg 2012 gives an argument for thinking that there is an asymmetry of reference.
4   This is ambiguous. It could mean that causation makes it the case that if you have some state of a system, the system will have some particular state as the next one. Or it could mean that causation is the thing that means that there is a next state at all. I think causation does both of these, but the first one is the widely accepted one. And when I say 'next', it needn't be the very next (as we saw in chapter 2, there may be no such state) but merely the next one we are interested in.
5   Strap in...
6   I often find this thought a little depressing. Every time I tidy my house, making it more ordered, effectively what I am doing is expending lots of energy to move the disorder to somewhere else, such as the rubbish dump. I once got told off by someone's mother for telling her son this, when he complained about having to tidy his room. If it helps, biological life is a guerrilla war against entropy; we are only putting off the inevitable decomposition of our well-organised physical bodies, but between now and the inevitable is when all the fun happens.
7   Sometimes we see the puddles freeze, or atmospheric moisture form pretty snowflakes, but those aren't the same.
8   Actually, *supposing* the world to be convenient is probably sensible, provided if, when you test your supposition, you revise the supposition if the test doesn't confirm the convenience of the world.

9 Woodward (2005) argues for this.
10 Beebee (2000) describes the difference between the best systems view of causal laws and the alternative 'governing' view.

FURTHER READING

For a defence of the past hypothesis, Albert (2000) is very clear and accessible.
Horwich (1988) gives an overview of different asymmetries in time.
Baron, Miller, Tallant (2022) tries to convince you that, for all you know, there is no time, and not even enough time-like structure for the C-theory.

FATALISM

In the previous chapter we looked at a difference between past and future: the arrow of time. That was meant to explain various asymmetries between past and future, such as the asymmetry of records, the asymmetry of intervention, and differences of attitudes between past and future. In this chapter the worry is that the future might resemble the past more than we think. If the future is settled in the way the past is, what does that mean for us?

Occasionally you see headlines in popular science magazines like 'Scientists discover there is no free will!'. It might seem odd that that is the kind of thing that a scientist could discover. Nonetheless, it's clear that lots of people think that there is an important connection between our account of the nature of time (and the nature of the difference between past and future) and our attitudes towards actions we may or may not take. In this chapter, the aim is to tease apart some of the threads by which the nature of time is connected to action.

THE PAST IS SETTLED

The advice that there's no use crying over spilt milk is often deeply unhelpful. The point of crying is not generally its practical usefulness, but as an expression of distress, which is part of a system of social signalling that may reward or punish such expressions in various ways. The advice is usually an expression of impatience for expressions of distress. But the impatience seems to come from a widely held thought: you can't change the past, but you can do things about the future. In the case of spilt milk, you can clean it up

DOI: 10.4324/9781003189459-7

before it turns sour and starts to smell rancid; that way you won't have a rancid smell to cry about later. More generally the advice suggests that rather than having a futile wish to change past mistakes, resolve to make the future better.

In the previous chapter we introduced the asymmetry of intervention and the asymmetry of affect. The advice suggests that given the asymmetry of intervention (you can't do anything to undo your mistake) you should have a certain emotional response. The advice is bad, because the emotional response isn't related to the asymmetry of intervention in that way. Crying about milk you haven't yet spilt doesn't seem a *more* appropriate emotional response, particularly if it is still possible to prevent it being spilt.[1] Crying over actual spilt milk makes much more sense than crying over merely potentially spilt milk. Nonetheless, it is technically correct that crying over spilt milk does not assist with the (time-sensitive) activity of clearing up the milk.

Better advice is available. Confucius for example, said:

> One does not try to explain what is over and done with, one does not try to criticize what is already gone, and one does not try to censure that which is already past.[2]

And Ancient Greek Poet Agathon said:

> For even from god this power is kept, this power alone: To make it true that what's been done had never been.[3]

Across time and culture, it tends to be acknowledged that the past is settled, and that this has consequences for the way we navigate the world. We often can't do anything about the future, but we can never do anything about the past.[4] Ignoring time travel for a moment (which we will consider in chapter 11), let's accept that the past is settled, and that this has consequences for our emotional responses to the world, our attitudes and our decisions. Now let's consider how we would be affected if there were no asymmetry of intervention? What if the future were settled too? I'm going to use the term 'fatalism' to describe the idea that the future might be settled, and that this has bad consequences for how we act in and feel about the world. We'll be looking at a variety of different fatalistic worries, and thinking about which ones are worrisome and why.

IS THE FUTURE SETTLED?

There are a bunch of ways in which the future might be settled:

- There are a complete set of truths about the future.
- There's some divine entity that has plans for the future, and what happens in the future is dictated by that entity.
- The universe operates on deterministic causal laws.
- The future is just as real as this time, but located somewhere else.

I'll explain what these are, and why they are different from each other. It might be that the future is settled in some of these ways and not others.

FUTURE TRUTH

If future truth is settled it means that there's a single description of how things will be in the future that is true and that will not change. We need to be a little bit careful here about what we mean when we say 'will be true'. I want to distinguish between the claim that when the future becomes present it *will* have a complete set of truths, and the claim that there are is a complete set of truths (perhaps knowable by God, perhaps not) that describe how the future *will* be. The idea is that a description of the future might be completely settled, even if the future hasn't happened yet.

The 'Lazy Argument for Fatalism' is a terrible argument, but it is useful in framing some of the less terrible ones later. We take some unknown feature of the future and we reason about it, showing that you don't need to change your action based on it.

1. You will either pass your exams or you won't.
2. If you're going to pass your exams, there's no need to do revision; it's redundant.
3. If you're not going to pass your exams, there's no need to do revision; it's ineffective.

C. There's no need to do revision.

I told you the argument is terrible. Whether or not you will pass depends on what you do before the exam. Believing there are truths about the future doesn't commit you to thinking that they will be true *regardless of what happens*. If you think there are truths about the future, it will usually be that this is because there are also truths about whatever those truths depend on. If it is true that you will pass your exams, it may be true because it's also true that you will do revision.

In classical logic, for every statement, that statement is either true or false (but not both). This could mean that there is a single set of truths that describe how the future will be, with everything that will happen being described by a true statement, and every description that fails to describe something that will happen being false. And then you can say that these descriptions never change.

You needn't think that classical logic gives you an unchanging picture though. Patrick Todd (2021) argues that all 'future contingents' (i.e. statements about how things will be that are not true simply because of logic) are false. So, according to Todd, it's false that you will pass your exams, and it's false that you will not pass your exams. (But true that you either will or you won't.)

But you might think that statements about the future don't need to be settled in that way. You might think that statements about the future can be neither true nor false. So, it's not true that you will pass your exams and not false (but true that you will pass them or you will not pass them).[5] One of the responses to the prospect of future truth being settled is to describe ways in which future truth is unsettled, modifying the logic we use as necessary. We aren't forced to think that there must be a complete unchangeable description of how the future will be just because statements must be true or false in classical logic.

How much of a problem would it be if there were (unknown to us) truths about how the future will be? It's not obvious that truths by themselves are especially worrying. That they are unknown is unhelpful, but being able to accurately predict the future is often really useful. If you were in an exam where every time you pressed a button on your calculator an unpredictable sequence of lines came up on the screen, that would make the calculator unusable, and throw you off your game.[6] We'll consider the case where you have perfect information later, but the mere existence of truths doesn't seem so worrying. We might wonder where they came from, however.

DIVINE PLAN

The origin of the word 'fate' is the Latin for 'that which has been spoken'. The idea is that someone has a prophecy, and some being or group of beings has arranged things so that you will fulfil the prophecy. It might be that this is regardless of what you do, but often it's that what you do has already been accounted for. Your attempts to evade the prophesy are in fact *exactly* the circumstances required to fulfil it.

There's a prophecy that Oedipus will marry his mother and kill his father, so he gets taken to a different country. But it's only because he later meets them as strangers that the prophecy is fulfilled. This kind of fatalistic worry is difficult because there is a plan, and even when you are making decisions for yourself, you are an instrument in someone else's plan. Let's call this scenario 'Divine Plan'.

Many cultures have a role for divine prophesies. The word '*inshallah*', meaning 'God willing' has entered English from Arabic, and is used to express hope that an uncertain enterprise may succeed. The Yoruba creator of life, *Oludamare*, is thought by believers to choose a future for them, and the westward expansion of the USA in the 19th century was based on the belief that it was the 'manifest destiny' of Americans to settle across the breadth of the North American continent.

CAUSAL DETERMINATION

Suppose the state of the universe at some past time and the laws of nature only leave a single possibility for how the future will go.[7] Call this claim 'Determinism'. Determinism gets you the future truths being settled, but not by ignoring dependencies on other things. Quite the reverse. Everything you will ever do, ever think and ever feel is a consequence of the positions and velocities of the particles in the universe before you were born. There need not be any agent with a plan. And in the Divine Plan case, there need not be deterministic laws. If the planner(s) are divine, they might arrange for some miracles that violate the normal laws.

Peter Van Inwagen (1983) has an argument that says if the laws of nature are deterministic, since you had no choice about the positions and velocities of particles before you were born, and you have no choice about the laws of nature that determine what will happen, you have no choice about any future truths.

This is the classic 'free will versus determinism' problem. I'm not going to talk about it much. There are plenty of discussions of it elsewhere, and it doesn't have much to do with time that is interesting. I mention it mainly to say 'this isn't the fatalistic worry we're interested in'.

But while we're here and I'm being grumpy about it, here are a couple of thoughts. It's not clear what 'free will' means. There are a few things it might mean, some of which it's really implausible that humans could ever have, some of which are obviously nothing to do with Determinism, and some of which are obviously nothing to do with moral responsibility. It's hard to come up with a version of the notion which is realistic for creatures like us, concerns the possibility of moral responsibility and depends on the question of whether Determinism is true. It seems like a secular hangover from the Divine Plan worry, but I'm not sure it makes sense without the divine planner.

We can dismiss one reading of the tension between free will and determinism quickly: things happening *randomly* wouldn't make free will any different to things happening deterministically. It's just a mistake to confuse freedom and unpredictability. Radioactive decay is not an expression of free will, and many of the most morally responsible people I know are very predictable. In fact, that they can be relied on to do the responsible thing is part of what makes them morally good.

Here's the closest I can get to a worry about determinism. If we knew exactly how the future would go, we would find that our knowledge would undermine our ability to reason about it. We couldn't do a good job of making decisions if we knew in advance what those decisions would be. This is because decision making involves open-mindedness about the outcome. I'll come back to this case later.

EXISTENCE/ACTUALITY

Finally, let's think about the future this way. We are not worried about a plan or prophecy, and we're not worried about deterministic laws.

Let's imagine that the laws are chancy, and that there's no big plan. Nonetheless, you might think that the future is just as real as this time, just located somewhere else.

Presumably you are located somewhere right now. And presumably that's not the only place you have ever been. But the other places aren't any less real just because you are not there now, right? If you defend a static view, you might think other times are just other locations in a similar way to other places. Your birth and death are equally happening in a pair of regions equally real as the region containing you reading this sentence. They are just different locations to each other.[8] But – and this is the important bit – none of them are more real or more fully happening on the static view.

One of the best literary explorations of this view is Kurt Vonnegut's novella *Slaughterhouse Five*. It features some aliens, the Tralfamadorians, who experience time as we would experience the Rocky Mountains.[9] From their point of view, we are, at each moment, 'trapped, like a bug in amber'. As a consequence, they lack any asymmetry of affect. About any event, at any point in time, they say 'so it goes'. If this response to time is warranted by any of the views we have considered, they will count as fatalistic worries.

Having laid out the different candidate worries, let's think a little about the historical context of the problem.

STOIC FATALISTIC THINKING

Though issues of fate and prophecy are to be found in a number of cultures, the contemporary Western philosophical debate owes a lot to the Ancient Greek and Roman Stoics. In particular there are two concepts of freedom to tease apart. There are the things which 'depend on us'.[10] And there is 'self-mastery'; the freedom from external influence that is characteristic of a free citizen rather than a slave.[11] It's going to be useful to keep these two concepts separate.

The Stoics were a school of Ancient Greek Philosophers named after the *Stoa Poikile* in Athens. This was a covered walkway on the edge of the main public square in ancient Athens, where Zeno of Citium (not to be confused with the Zeno of Elea from chapter 2) defended his philosophical views. Stoicism was popular in Ancient Greece and then Ancient Rome up until Christianity became the official religion of the Roman Empire. It has had a number of revivals in the West, particularly when people are looking for alternative ways of thinking to Christianity. At its heart is the idea that there's a difference between what is beyond your control and what depends on you. You can only be responsible for what depends on you, Stoics argue. So, Stoicism makes some pretty important claims about what the world is like independent of you, and what depends on you.

One popular Stoic analogy is that you are like a dog tied to a cart. Your choice is to follow behind the cart, or be dragged. But you have no choice about what the cart will do. For Stoics, you have no choice over things beyond your control, only over your responses. And almost everything is beyond your control. The Ancient Stoics believed that there were truths about the future, that these truths were causally determined now and in the past, and that this was part of a Divine Plan. In fact, they believed that time was circular, so the near future was also the distant past, and we were just moving through this cycle. In our responses, then, we should avoid getting excited by nice things happening, or become sad by unpleasant things happening, because we were just sequentially occupying different positions in the cycle, and neither success nor failure depended on us.

This rather crude summary of Stoicism met with objections even in Ancient Greece. If everything is fated, how can *anything*, even our responses, depend on us? Roughly, the answer the Stoics gave is, because the distinction between external causes and that which depends on us is not the same as the distinction between what is causally determined and what is not. When we decide upon a course of action, we may be causally influenced by things external to us, but what we do depends on our character, and psychology, and not just on things external to us. That our character and psychology were themselves caused to be the way they are is simply irrelevant for the distinction between external causes and what depends on us.

The idea here is that there is a really important distinction between different explanations of why we do something. If someone grabs your arm, and uses it to hit someone else, the other person getting hit did not depend on you; it depended on the person who had grabbed your arm. If someone tells you a series of lies that suggest that a person has gravely insulted you, and you punch them on the nose, then punching them depends on you *and* on the other person. You are not merely an instrument that they are hitting someone with, but a rational agent responding to reasons. But this talk about reasons doesn't mean that there weren't also causes. It means that the kinds of moral explanation we want to give depends on reasons rather than causes. Concepts like 'offence' are going to feature in the explanation of why you punched them, where they just wouldn't make sense in an explanation of how someone used your arm to hit someone. That which depends on us involves responding to reasons, and allows for us to attribute praise or blame. This is a different type of activity to giving causal/mechanical explanations.

In addition to what's up to us, the Stoics have an ideal of 'self-mastery',[12] where we are not slaves to our emotions. Someone who has self-mastery, in this sense, is master of their emotions, and so is immune to persuasion by sad stories, propaganda, advertising or seduction. Equally, someone with self-mastery is immune to bribery, blackmail and threats. Someone with self-mastery can only be persuaded by logical argument, and never by mere appeals to emotion. For the early Stoics, at least, the ideal of self-mastery was something that very few humans were likely to achieve; only the 'sage', the wisest of people, had self-mastery in this sense. So any healthy reasonable adult can be held worthy of praise or blame for actions that depended on them, very few would be so in control of their feelings that they would achieve this higher standard of self-mastery. Later on, these two different concepts get run together, and we get worries that virtually no-one has sufficient self-mastery to be morally responsible at all. But that's not what interests us here.

In terms of fatalism, we get the worries from Stoicism that the gods have plans for us, and it is as if we are being dragged through good times and bad with no prospect of intervention on our successes or otherwise; only on our attitude. The future that we cannot predict is just the same as the past we cannot remember. We can no more change the future than we can control the past. Even if you command the whole Roman Empire, you can be struck down by illness or misfortune and it is the will of the gods whether your plans succeed or not.

As a contemporary audience we might object to a lot here. Many of us may not believe in gods that have plans for us, and whose will gets carried out. And we may reject the thought that the future that we can't predict is the same as the past we can't remember. Time as a giant circle where we return through the same pattern again and again may be a useful metaphor about the kinds of mistakes humans make, but very few would take this literally. What's more, many might be cautious about the ideal of being immune to emotional appeals. The stoics certainly weren't advocating hard-heartedness – not being overwhelmed by emotion is different to not caring about others! – but the aim of self-mastery can end up in practice with our holding ourselves and others to impossible standards.

FATALISTIC THINKING TODAY

Modern Stoicism is inspired by the ancient variety, and is often practiced as part of a self-help movement, and is the inspiration for various mental-health treatments such as Rational-Emotive Behavioural Therapy (REBT) and Cognitive Behavioural Therapy (CBT). Modern Stoicism isn't tied to Stoic views of nature. It doesn't require the gods having a plan, or nature being a big cycle we are being carried through. It's not clear, then, that modern stoics are committed to fatalism in the way the ancient stoics were.

Nonetheless, fatalistic thinking is still present in the contemporary world. We often see fatalistic thinking in attempts to console each other; 'If it wasn't meant to be, it wasn't meant to be', 'What's for you will not go by you', 'God has a plan for you', etc. These are appeals to a Divine Plan.

As an aside, there is lots of evidence that fatalistic thinking of this kind is associated with people being less healthy or dying sooner. Various studies find that people with these beliefs are less likely to use safety precautions, and more likely to engage in risky behaviours.[13] It would be a mistake to conclude from this that fatalistic beliefs are *causing* risky behaviours, or failure to use safety precautions, since it could be that some prior trauma, for example, is causing both the fatalistic beliefs and the risky behaviour.

We also often find fatalistic thinking in contemporary physics. Rather than in the form of a Divine Plan, it comes in a claim that the future is just another location separated from this one in a time-like direction rather than a space-like one. What happens in the future is just as real a feature of the physics as what happened in the past and what is happening right now. The difference is just in our knowledge. We can directly observe what is happening nearby right now, and we have access to records of the past, but we cannot observe, directly or through records, what is going to happen in the future.

On such views, the future is different from past and present only in terms of our access to information about it, but not in whether it exists, or whether anything is happening there. Each time seems like it is happening to the people at that time, but all times are equally real/actual/happening. But the connection between the equal status of different times to the undermining of our decisions depending on us, or our being morally responsible is unclear. This view is different from causal determinism. You can hold either one without holding the other. But I think that we should worry about treating the future as being just as real as the past in a way we shouldn't worry about causal determination. For the remainder of the chapter, I will survey the different ways that we might worry about the future being settled.

FATALISM AND INFORMATION

Does knowing what is going to happen undermine your ability to be responsible for your actions? It might be true that if you know what is going to happen you will act differently than you otherwise would. You might not attempt to do things that you know to be impossible, for example. But knowing what you are going to do doesn't seem to stop you doing it. Indeed, predicting something is going to happen is often part of intending that something will happen. When we carry out actions, we often expect to succeed in the action that we are attempting.

There are also cases where, despite knowing what's going to happen, we try to make it not happen. This might not be rational. If we *know* we will fail, there's no point in trying. But often we are vulnerable to wishful thinking. Wishful thinking isn't a good thing. In fact, we are often blameworthy for acting in the face of the available evidence. But the fact that we are blameworthy suggests that we are still *responsible* for our actions.

It might be that it is often more helpful not to know what's going to happen. We might find it oppressive, or distracting. It might even make us feel like we are not able to shape the stories of our lives because we are living a story that has been pre-written. But we praise an actor who performs a scripted play for their performance. So, it's not that information about the future undermines the possibility of praise or blame, though it might change the way we feel about events.

FATALISM AND BEING AN INSTRUMENT

If what's going to happen is someone else's plan, that seems to affect our attitudes towards it. If you find out you have been manipulated into doing something, you might revisit whether you were responsible for your actions.

Imagine you work for a large organisation, and your employer asks you to do a particular task. You have to deal with an unhappy customer, for example. Let's imagine it's a customer you've never had any dealings with before – it wasn't you who made them unhappy. They might object to what you do when you are following the instructions your employer gave you. It can be tempting to think you are not responsible for your actions; your employer bears responsibility. But it's not clear that this is how responsibility works. It seems like it's much easier to multiply than it is to get rid of. Your employer is responsible for your actions, since you are acting on behalf of the company. But you are also responsible for your actions, since you are the person carrying them out. You have not ceased to have moral responsibility just because you have been told to carry out an instruction.

This seems to carry over to cases of manipulation. If someone manipulates you, you are still responsible for your actions, even if they are responsible for manipulating you. If people could be reasonably expected to achieve Stoic self-mastery, then we might think it is solely their fault for getting manipulated. But given that virtually no-one achieves that, it's possible to be responsible for how we respond to manipulation and to hold whoever manipulates responsible for manipulating others.

If we make the manipulator divine rather than human, it doesn't seem to change things much. We are still responsible for our actions and they for theirs. But when we think about manipulation, we might think that everyone isn't equal. When those in positions of authority manipulate those they have power over, we think it's important to acknowledge the differences in power. If the people in question are very young, or drunk, or on drugs, or tired or hungry, we don't hold them responsible in the same way we do if they are none of those things. Holding people responsible is a bit more complicated than deciding *whether* someone is responsible or not. If there is a Divine Plan, planned by a being much better informed and much more powerful than us, it may change how we think about praise and blame significantly.

FIXTURES AND OPTIONS

You might worry that for us to be morally responsible, we need to be able to deliberate amongst options. If we aren't choosing from amongst a range of options, we can't be held responsible for our 'choice'. It's not really a choice if there aren't options to choose between. If you think this, then determinism needn't be a problem for responsibility, simply because we don't know what we will choose. There are a bunch of options, and although only one of them is what will happen, we don't know which that is, since we are weighing up reasons and deciding on a particular outcome. Even if this is all inevitable, we can be held morally responsible because the required deliberative process has taken place.

You can't deliberate properly if you know in advance of a deliberation what outcome you will choose. It's simply not a deliberation if you have made up your mind from the start. So you have to enter a deliberation, the argument goes, without knowing what you are going to decide.

This argument amounts to the claim that you need to *think* you have multiple options. It's fine if there are not multiple options, so long as you don't know that. If you had better knowledge of the future, you would not be able to deliberate, because you would know what you are going to do and there would be nothing to deliberate over.

On this view, it's not the causal determination, a Divine Plan, or the existence/actuality of the future that is relevant to fatalism, but *information*. If you know what's going to happen, you are not able to deliberate, and so cannot make decisions about the future. You can only deliberate about things that you take to be *options*, not things that you take to be *fixtures*.

One thing that is worth thinking carefully about here is the relationship between deliberation and decision making. Often when we think about making decisions, we think about weighing up of various courses of action and comparing them. But sometimes making decisions doesn't involve any deliberation; we know what to do straightaway. Indeed, we often talk about decisions that don't involve choice. A judge issuing a sentence might say 'I have no choice but to recommend a custodial sentence'. The judge is still responsible for issuing the sentence, they just don't think the decision was a finely balanced one. It's not clear that we need to think there is more than one option to make a decision, even if we need more than one option to deliberate. In order to make a decision we do need *at least* one option. So we can make a decision to do the thing that is our only option, but if we have no options at all, there is no decision to take.

It may well be true that people prefer to have (a small number of) options to choose between. If we believed that we knew exactly how the future was going to go, it might affect our emotional state, and lead to apathy. But this might not be the same as an inability to make decisions or to be responsible for them.

Notice that making the issue about information, rather than about the status of the future, changes the debate. Fatalism becomes an issue about people's attitudes, and not about the nature of time.

EXISTENCE AND ACTUALITY

Suppose we accept that there is only one way the future can go, and we know what it is. Does it make any difference if the future 'exists'?

One difficulty in answering this question is that we've run straight into the thorny question of what 'existence' means. Here's another way of putting the question: Think of a place, perhaps the location of someone you know well, that is not the same as the place you currently are. In fact, you can't see or hear each other. Even though you are not there, you might think that there's nothing special about the place you are compared to the place they are. Both places are just as real, even though you can only currently experience one of them. Are the past and the future like that? Are they just as real as this place, even though you aren't there?

You might think that other times *are* just like other places. Or you might think other times are importantly different. Nothing is happening in the past, because it is already over and done with, and nothing is happening in the future, because it's not begun yet. You might think that the future is still something that *could* happen, or perhaps *will* happen, but that's just not the same as saying it has happened somewhere else.

One way of thinking about this is that the change from future to present to past is a change from potential to actual. The future is potential, the past is actual, and the present, when stuff happens, is a change from potential to actual.[14] If what it is to be present is to be changing in this way, there must be some potential to change into something actual. If the future is just like the present, this process of change from potential to actual can't take place. You just have a series of actual things separated in time. Instead of 'potential' and 'actual' we could talk about existing and not existing. If the future exists, an event can't come into existence as it takes place.

This change from potential to actual, or from not existing to existing doesn't require there being many potential futures. It can take place even in a deterministic universe (and in one where there is a Divine Plan, and in which people have complete information). But it gives a sense in which the future must be unsettled to make sense of anything whatever happening.

If this view is right, deliberation, decisions, actions, and thoughts all depend on a process of changing what could/would be into what is. But if you think that this kind of change is needed to make sense of action, you might think that a world in which past, present and future were all equally existing/actual would be one in which we could not make sense of action (whether up to us or not). It would be a world in which it wouldn't make sense to describe anything as happening.

Why should we believe in this change? This kind of view builds quite a lot into the nature of time; much more than physics seems to require. Part of the motivation for this account is to make sense of the asymmetries discussed in the previous chapter: the asymmetries of intervention, of records, of reference and of affect. The change from potential to actual is the process of causation bringing things about. Part of it has to do with McTchange. We are aware of experiencing a sequence of events in succession. This sequence is, for the most part, reasonably orderly and doesn't seem to be under our control.

We can't change what day it is as easily as we can change which city we're in. If we like a city, we can choose to stay there longer, but if we like a day, we can't make it last longer.

The change in what exists, or in what is actual, is meant to explain not just the arrow of time, but the fact that time keeps passing whether we like it or not. But if you think that this experience of change in what day it is can be explained in terms of information available to us, rather than because of the nature of time, the appeal to a change in existence or actuality will seem extravagant. One puzzle, however, is that if this is to be explained in terms of information, we still need to explain the change in our informational state. If we look at a series of snapshots of our informational state, we might be able to explain the difference between past and future directions, and why we would notice change. But it's puzzling to make sense of living through a series of such snapshots, if they are just an unchanging sequence of perspectives.

QUESTIONS FOR DISCUSSION

1. Is it just humans who have actions that are up to them?
2. Does it make any difference whether the future is settled if we don't know what it will be?
3. If the future is settled, does it make any difference whether this was because of Divine Plan?
4. If we had as much information about the future as we do about the past, how would that affect our ability to make choices about our actions?
5. If the future is just another place, do the people there matter morally in just the same way as people where you are?

NOTES

1 There's something particularly unfortunate about the emotional response to something unpleasant that's going to happen, because often the emotional response to the prospect makes it more likely. Being really worried that you will make a mistake is likely to make you more nervous, which makes mistakes more likely. These situations are known as self-fulfilling prophesies. The usefulness of emotional responses is often at odds with whether they are appropriate evaluations of the situation.

2 Confucius *Analects* 3.21, trans. Slingerland

3 Aristotle *Nicomachean Ethics* 1139b10, trans. Christopher Rowe

4 Let's continue to ignore the cases where the past itself depends on how the future will go.

5 In Briggs and Forbes (2012) we discuss three different options for this, but be warned this paper gets into technical issues of logic.

6 It certainly did in my case.

7 See e.g. Van Inwagen (1983)

8 If you are reading this on your deathbed, then what I just said will not be true. I apologise for my presumption, an offer my commiserations on your circumstances.

9 We considered our first-personal experience as of endurance in chapter 4. The Tralfamadorians don't have that.

10 Greek: *eph'hēmin*

11 Greek: *eleutheria*

12 Greek: *eleutheros*

13 E.g. Kayani, King and Fleiter (2012)

14 This is a view that I defend in Forbes (2016) by the way.

FURTHER READING

Bobzein (2021) goes into the history of Stoic ideas of freedom.

Zagzebski (2015) presents a puzzle for getting the arrow of time to create a fatalistic worry.

Fernandes (2019) looks at the asymmetry of affect, and argues that we can't go from an asymmetry of affect to a dynamic view of time.

TIME TRAVEL

We've been talking largely about time as we ordinarily encounter it. We've touched a little on the challenges of very small scales, where quantum phenomena affect things, and very large scales, where relativity becomes a central concern. But in popular culture, if you talk about the philosophy of time, one phrase isn't far from people's minds: 'time travel'. It's a staple of science fiction, from H.G. Wells (1895) to Audrey Niffenegger (2003) and F.M.A. Dixon (2022).

One technicality to get clear on straight-away: when we ask if time travel is possible, it is time travel to the past that we are primarily interested in. Time travel to the future is quite straightforward: it is also known as 'waiting'. It may be that if we travel at near-light speeds, or approach a concentration of mass like a black hole, the relativistic effects will mean that we age slower compared to our twin; the clocks measuring our travel through time may measure less than clocks that did not go on that journey. But in terms of travelling from A to B, that's just a matter of journey time. As Peter Van Inwagen (2010:3) observes: 'I suppose that even the chair I am sitting on can be regarded as a limiting case of a machine for travel to the future: if I sit on it long enough, shall find myself in 2071.'

It is time travel to the past, then, that this chapter will be concerned with.

TRAVEL TO THE PAST

Time travel is a complicated business. You've got someone entering some kind of vehicle – a *time machine* – and leaving at a different time. So far, that description is satisfied by any vehicular travel, and

DOI: 10.4324/9781003189459-8

could be satisfied by climbing into a box, waiting and climbing out. With time travel to the past, they enter the vehicle and then leave it *earlier* than they entered. But earlier for whom? If someone leaves a vehicle earlier than they enter it, that's not time travel; that's just returning to a vehicle. For time travel we need a situation in which someone enters a vehicle and then later *from their point of view* leaves it again, but *from the point of view of an observer* they leave the vehicle and then later enter it.

David Lewis (1976) suggests a distinction between *external time* and *personal time*. For a non-time-traveller, personal time and external time are just the same. But in the case of the time traveller, personal time is time from their point of view, and external time is time from a non-time traveller's point of view.

This distinction isn't a distinction between 'objective' time and 'experienced' or 'lived' time. Both personal and external time are objective: they are supposed to be the sort of time that clocks measure. It's just that the time traveller's clock undergoes a different series of events to the observer's clock. We can represent these as two dimensions on a simple graph, as in Figure 11.1.

As we can see, Figure 11.1 involves someone initially traveling normally through time (as represented by an increase in external

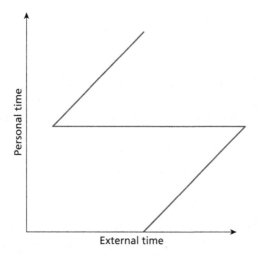

Figure 11.1 A journey through time

time at the same rate as they increase in personal time). They then travel back in external time (as represented by the horizontal line), followed by travelling forward in time as normal.

I have assumed that a vehicle is involved, simply for practicality. Because one of the problems for time travel is working out what goes to the past. How does the time-travel device know what to send? A special vehicle is a helpful way of containing all the relevant stuff inside. Send too much stuff and there will be waste and damage. Think of the fragments of flooring and furniture! Send too little, and the traveller will find that they have stuff missing when they arrive. Time travel that removes your feet is not to be recommended.

While we're considering practical issues, I wish to lodge a complaint. When depicted in fiction, time travel is unrealistically straightforward. Consider the huge effort that went into the space-race over the course of decades. That level of research and development is not something that could be done from someone's garage. What's more, a series of tests would be needed to establish proof-of-concept. Compared to time travel, space travel is a safe and straightforward affair.

PRACTICAL ISSUES

Assuming that you do successfully travel through time, there are a number of issues that a skilful science-fiction writer will deal with, avoid, or directly instruct the reader not to worry about.

Can you speak the language? The colloquialisms in use are often very culturally specific, and generational. Accents change quite quickly and 500 years out from your time or origin you may find it difficult to be understood. Even if you can understand the language, you'll be entering a society as a stranger. If the past is proverbially another country, in which they do things differently, you'll be a foreigner. How will they make sense of you? You may be wearing strange clothes, have a strange haircut, and be unprepared for social expectations. Will you be arrested as a vagrant, or invited in as an honoured guest? What social class will you belong to? Before the 17th century, laws used to regulate who could wear what materials and what colours. Will your presence invite people to view you as someone to be robbed, or someone to be feared? Will you be accused of witchcraft? Solving the engineering problem is only half the battle; the anthropological challenges are at least as great.

You will have to take most of what you need with you. Spare parts will be impossible to come by, as will synthetic materials. So many features of modern technology are incredibly recent. Transistors were a 20th century invention, and electric motors were invented in the 19th century. There may be no internet, and no Wikipedia before 2001.

Landing in the right place matters. The earth is revolving, orbiting the sun, and also orbiting the centre of gravity of the earth and moon. Relativistic physics makes the idea of being in the 'same place' at a different time as difficult as being at the 'same time' in a different bit of space was when we discussed relativity in chapter 5. But the bit of space–time you intend to go to will probably be moving relative to your starting point. Getting it so you land on the surface of a planet without burning up in the atmosphere, or creating a huge crater is not often addressed.

Surviving the journey is also a consideration. Astronauts have to cope with gravitational forces in the spacecraft to escape the earth's gravity. But the forces involved for time travel may well be fatal for any organism. The temperatures need to avoid either boiling or freezing your blood, and you need to avoid changes in pressure that lead to altitude sickness or decompression sickness.[1] Once you arrive, you will most likely be highly contagious to whomever you meet, and will probably catch some disease that you have no resistance to yourself. Time travel is a serious business.

When it comes to practical issues, the big ones are political ones. If time travel becomes a regular thing, the issues of exploration, invasion, exploitation of resources, colonisation, integration, oppression, immigration and self-determination that apply for travel between places become issues. Difficult ones to resolve, no doubt.

One alternative is to send a message instead. Sending information, for example in binary code, seems much more plausible than sending a person. It might be that Morse code is an option, as previously used by telegraph operators and naval signallers with flashing lights. You could send a positively charged particle for a • and negatively charged one for a ■, for example.

BACKWARDS CAUSATION

If we accept that time travel is possible, does that mean that backwards causation is possible? We need to be a little careful in how we phrase things here. What is it to cause something to happen in the past?

We might distinguish between *changing* the past and *affecting* the past. Changing the past seems to suggest that there was a way the past was, that is then altered. We might think it is impossible to change the past for the same reason it is impossible to change the future. When I change my mind about what to have for lunch tomorrow, I don't change the future. It's not that the future was previously determinate in a particular way and now it is determinate in another way. It was simply never the case that the future contained the now aborted plan coming to fruition. Similarly, it is not that the past was one way and now the past is a different way. It might be that the past was previously indeterminate and now has become determinate, or it might be that the past contained the result of time travel all along.

The issue here is that the past cannot be different to itself. The past is the stuff that happened. If it gets changed, it simply ceases to be the *past*. If someone travels back in time and then does things that didn't happen in the original past, they haven't changed the past but have created a new event which is not on the same timeline as the one they travelled back from. (See Figure 11.2.) The timeline may have branched to create a new timeline (which is past from *someone's* point of view). But this new event isn't earlier in external time (it's on a different timeline) and isn't earlier in personal time (it's later). It might become the past after the time-traveller goes there, but only in the sense that the future always becomes the past after it's present.

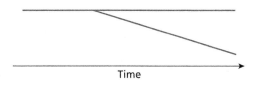

Time

Figure 11.2 A branching timeline

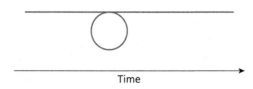

Time

Figure 11.3 A causal loop

Even if you can't change your own past, you might be able to affect it. 'Affecting' your past merely requires that you are a causal influence on it. This is compatible with it being the past that causally led to your travelling back in time. This is because you could be in a **causal loop**. A causal loop has the feature that, when you are inside the loop, your personal past and future are the same. (See Figure 11.3.) If you go back far enough in personal time, you get to your personal present again.[2]

One of the big challenges for making sense of causal loops is the *first time around* problem. Suppose you set off in your time machine into your own past. What caused you to do that? There was a sequence of events that led to you stepping into the machine and turning it on. Included in that sequence of events, was your stepping out of a time machine and interacting with various things. What caused you to step out of the machine to interact with various things? Your stepping into the machine some years later and travelling back in time! There's no first version where you've not made it to the past yet that gets the cycle going. The cycle doesn't have a beginning or an end.

I said this was a problem, but I've just re-described a causal loop. The problem can't simply be that a causal loop is a causal loop! That's not a very good explanation of why it would be a problem. But the thought seems to be that originating actions is pretty important for being morally responsible for things, and causal loops seem to involve lots of actions, but some of them aren't *originated*. And it's hard to make sense of these.

Suppose I send a copy of this book into the past, and suggest a clever moneymaking scheme: past me copies the book into a new file, and sends it to the publishers. I know the scheme will work, because it has already worked, and I remember doing it. The publisher publishes it, and gives me a complimentary copy. I send the complimentary copy into the past, completing the causal loop. Here's the problem: no-one writes the book!

The story I just told doesn't at any stage involve anyone writing the book. It involves me plagiarising the book, but never writing it. I don't write it, but nor does anyone else. Nonetheless, there is this book, as real as the one you are now reading, that never got written. Who deserves the credit/blame for writing the book? Not me; I didn't write it! But it doesn't seem to make sense that we could have a book that never gets written. It exists, fully formed, with no process of coming to be, just a perpetual change from published book to manuscript and back. We couldn't explain why the book said what it did, simply that it always says what it says. If I attempted to change the content of the book, correcting errors and such, I wouldn't succeed (at least not without breaking the causal loop and starting a new timeline) since the errors are the ones that get published and that are included in the copy that I go on to have already sent back.

Causal loops are very strange. But they are yet stranger still. Because according to the standard geometry of relativistic physics, they are physically possible. **Closed Time-like Curves** as they are known, are paths through space–time where a journey is continually made in a time-like direction (relative to the changing inertial frame of the traveller) that eventually intersects with a point in space–time 'earlier' in the journey. The fact that the mathematics of relativity allows for them doesn't mean that they are physically possible, but it is pretty striking that they are not clearly physically impossible either.

THE GRANDFATHER PARADOX

Suppose that you have a time machine and can travel back in time. What can you do when you get to the past? In theory, you can do anything that you could do in the present, because it's the present when you get there. But some things that might seem really straightforward physically possible acts turn out to be things that you have no chance of doing.

Suppose you travel back in time and attempt to do something that affects the past such that you don't get born. Given that you did get born, that would lead to a single timeline in which you are both born at some time and never born. That is a contradiction. You might think that contradictions cannot actually happen.[3] Nonetheless, given that your grandfather was a biological creature with the usual vulnerabilities, shooting him before he conceived your father (or mother) is hardly a miraculous sequence of events. The puzzle about whether it is possible to travel back in time to kill one's own grandfather is known as the **grandfather paradox**.[4] Grandparents aren't strictly required, any situation in which you act so as to prevent your own existence will count as a grandfather paradox.

One response to the grandfather paradox is that we need to separate out the claim that you *can* kill your grandfather, from the claim that you *do* kill your grandfather. Of course you can kill him! You have the ability to acquire, load, aim and fire a gun. He is noticeably not bullet-proof. Shooting him in one of the vital organs would certainly be enough to kill him. It's just that, as it happens, you *don't* kill him. There are all sorts of things that you *could* do, but *won't* do. And in this case the things that you won't do are also things that you *didn't* do.

Suppose you *try*. If you try to do things you can do, you usually succeed. There's supposed to be some connection between the ability to do something, attempting to do something, and succeeding in doing that thing. If you fail to do something every time you try, eventually we would have to conclude that you are unable to do that thing. So, of course, if you tried you would probably succeed, provided there wasn't something that got in the way. Imagine you are taking careful aim, you have your grandfather in your sights, and then, just as you pull the trigger, your grandfather slips on a banana skin and falls over, taking him out of your line of fire. This doesn't undermine your ability to kill someone with a gun; this particular someone just had a lucky escape.

Suppose you try again, and the gun jams. Suppose you try a third time and it turns out that it wasn't your grandfather after all, but another time traveller attempting to kill Hitler that you've just killed. Whatever you do, it's certain that there will be *something* that prevents you succeeding. You are perfectly *able*, of course. You just don't succeed. Philosophers term the thing, whatever it is, that happens to prevent you succeeding 'a banana skin'. If you attempt to kill your grandfather, and you are in a causal loop, there *will* be a banana skin. Why? Because there *was* one when you attempted it in your own past.

David Lewis (1981) argued that we can understand the grandfather paradox in roughly this way. The laws of nature are such that the time traveller has the relevant ability, but the way things actually go is such that they don't use it. Stephanie Rennick (2015) points out a consequence of this: ordinary people have these abilities, but philosophers, who know there will always be a banana skin, can't have those abilities. This is because you cannot rationally intend to do something that you know will not succeed, and you know there will be a banana skin.

Causal loops are puzzling because they seem to be very robust (there is precisely one way things go) and very fragile (the smallest change would destroy the causal loop). Sometimes people talk about the 'butterfly effect'. This is the idea that, in a chaotic system, a small change in the conditions at one time leads to a large change in the conditions at another.[5] The effect is named after the idea that weather systems, despite being based on easily definable laws of motion, are incredibly hard to predict. A butterfly flapping its wings on one side of the world can cause a hurricane on the other. In time travel cases, a small change in the timing of a meeting can cause a chain of events that leads to an entirely different sequence of events unfolding. This sensitivity to small changes isn't anything to do with chance. Systems that are deterministic can be chaotic.

If the laws of nature are indeterministic, and allow for chance, there's an extra problem. Suppose you have two chancy events that are causally separated but that take place at the same time.[6] Let's imagine two coin tosses on either side of the planet. Suppose you were unsatisfied with the result of one coin toss and travelled back in time to give it another go. It being a chancy event, you may get a different result. But what about the other coin toss? Does that happen the same way it previously did, or not? One thought is that if it is genuinely chancy, it doesn't get held fixed either. If the universe is indeterministic, it's incredibly unlikely that travelling back to the past will result in the world evolving such that you enter a time machine in the right circumstances to travel back and complete the causal loop. You might be able to create a new timeline that branches off from your past, of course, but you won't have successfully travelled to your own past and changed that.

The difficulties in making sense of time travel should lead us to reflect on the different senses in which the future might be open discussed in chapter 7. Time travel seems to require the past to be open in whatever senses the future needed to be open to avoid fatalism. Either that, or time travel commits us to fatalism. If a time traveller is in a causal loop, should we think of them as *trapped* in that causal loop? It seems like it's different from mere determinism. It's not just that there are facts about what they will do, but those things have happened elsewhere.

THE MOVEABLE OBJECTIVE PRESENT

So far, our discussions of time travel 'to the past' have not discussed the status of the present. The distinction between external and personal time and the view of causal loops has entirely been set up in such a way that we can treat the terms 'past' and 'future' as being earlier/later than some observer's perspective. No McTchange has been assumed. But time travel gets even more interesting once we add the idea that there is a fact about what time is the objective present.

Sara Bernstein (2017) introduced the idea of a moveable objective present (MOP). This idea has two parts:

1. There is an objective present which can be manipulated.
2. A time-traveller can use their time machine to change the location of the objective present.

On this picture, time travel is a little more complicated than we have been assuming so far. It's not just a question of getting personal time to come apart from external time in the desired way, but of getting the MOP to go along with personal time.

Let's imagine the scenario: you step into your time machine, and set the controls for 1929. Perhaps you hope to prevent the Wall Street Crash. You activate the machine. Everything stops. In 1929, things roar into life. 1929 is the unique present at which things happen. *And* your time machine shows up. You have moved the MOP to a different location in external time, and moved your personal time so that it is where the MOP now is. Hopefully you've found a way of ensuring these happen together!

Let's think through some of the things that could go wrong.

	Traveller moves	Traveller stays
Present moves	Scenario A	Scenario C
Present stays	Scenario B	Scenario D

Scenario A looks like the good case: Both the MOP and the time traveller move. But do they move to the same time? If the traveller is earlier than where the MOP is, they are effectively dead on arrival. If they are later, they will be frozen there until the MOP catches up. Provided, of course, that the world still includes them when it gets there.

Scenario B is very bad for the traveller. They are effectively dead on arrival. There's no chance of the MOP catching up with them.

In Scenario C, the traveller might be OK, provided the world unfolds again so as to have them in it. If it evolves differently, they have effectively killed everyone at their own time.

Scenario D is potentially something of a disappointment. The traveller presses the button and no time travel happens. That's not to say nothing happens. Nothing happening would be a good outcome! If it was a genuine attempt at time travel, the quantities of energy involved would be staggering. One explanation for why neither the present nor the traveller moves might be because the entire machine blows up when the button gets pressed. Time travel with a MOP is a dangerous business!

Perhaps I'm being unfair to your time-travelling skill. You manage to get the time machine to relocate the moveable objective present and you to the same time. What happens to the rest of the world? Presumably they are all in the situation of the traveller in scenario C. They might be OK if the world evolves so as to include them. If not, they have all been killed.

Here's an alternative. The time machine, rather than moving the MOP, clones it and grafts it somewhere else, like a cutting from a plant. Time carries on outside the machine, and a new present (and perhaps a new timeline) starts branching off a previous time. That makes moving the present a less genocidal activity. It also means that you have multiple different presents going on, either in the same timeline or multiple different ones. This pushes us back into some metaphysical questions about what it is for something to be present, and in what respects the future needs to be open.

IS TIME-TRAVEL POSSIBLE?

Beyond its fascination for science-fiction writers, is time travel to the past possible? Closed time-like curves creating causal loops look like they are the best hope. They are compatible with relativity. The arrow of time is where the difficulties come in.

Suppose you think that the arrow of time is the entropic gradient. The causal loop doesn't increase in entropy as we would expect it to. If we take any point in the loop, we can treat that point as both the start and the end of a temporal sequence. But given it is the same point, its entropy will be the same at the start as at the finish. This looks to be difficult from the point of view of thermodynamics. But it is only a problem if it's a closed-system. If the causal loop is maintained by increasing entropy outside the causal loop, entropy still increases overall.

If, by contrast, the arrow of time is causal, backwards causation looks to be ruled-out from the start. After all, the direction of time just is the direction of causation on such a view. Closed time-like curves can be interpreted as involving a continuous loop of forwards causation, so the problem isn't so much *backwards* causation as having an event be causally upstream of itself and causally downstream of itself. The challenge with a causal arrow comes back to the issues of chapter 6 in what causation involves. If we have a best-systems view of causation, where causes are understood in terms of claims about what wouldn't have happened if some event hadn't happened, everything in the loop depends on everything else. It's difficult to explain what the direction of time is, on such a loop, but causally it's no problem.

If causation involves more *oomph*, that is, if it's a productive view of causation that involves making things happen, we have a question of how to understand *making things happen*. This was one of the difficult questions about it in the normal case, but whatever we say, we need to make sense of what it is for an event to happen in a causal loop. Things happening seems to be quite a linear business; one thing happens and then another. Loops, as we've seen above, are notable for neither having a beginning nor end. So, trying to describe them in terms of one thing happening after the other won't get us very far. This productive kind of causation seems to run into the first time around problem we discussed earlier.

If the arrow of time isn't simply a matter of entropy or causation, but of a modal change – a change from potentiality to actuality, or a change from non-existence to existence – time travel to the past is under more pressure still. If the arrow of time is a change from potentiality to actuality, or a change from non-existence to existence, those changes are either irreversible or reversible. If they are reversable, they don't play the role they are intended to in creating the arrow of time, and if they are irreversible, causal loops are ruled out. The same time cannot both be actual and potential. The same time cannot both exist and not exist.

Time travel potentially messes with things besides causation. Conceptually it would do a lot of damage. Travelling presupposes that the same individual leaves and arrives. Time travel requires **diachronic identity**. That is, it requires the traveller to survive.

Normally philosophical accounts of identity rely on *continuity*. Popular accounts of identity often have psychological continuity at their heart of physical continuity. If time travel involves discontinuities in external time we might have no way to establish what is personal time. The person that appears in 1929 attempting to avert the Wall Street Crash is not continuous, physically or psychologically, with anyone immediately before. Rather than searching the whole of space–time for someone they used to be, we could simply allow for the highly improbable possibility that the person popped into existence from nothing. It is highly improbable, but not impossible. Indeed, time travel to the past is improbable too. Perhaps it is more improbable than someone appearing from nowhere, and being convinced they are a time-traveller.

There are abstract worries about the possibilities of time travel, but if we noticed a series of phenomena that were best explained by time travel, our best theories would quickly make room for it. This leads to speculation about what sort of phenomena we would expect to find if time travel were possible.

For one thing, wouldn't we have records of people appearing unexpectedly, with strange tales about the future? Or, on a more realistic scenario, wouldn't we have messages from the future telling us things. A quick and unconvincing response is that maybe we do have records, but haven't been told. This response, beloved of conspiracy theorists, seems to presuppose the ability to keep some pretty significant secrets on behalf of the people who discovered it. It is not so much the malevolence of the authorities that I question, but their competence.

A somewhat more plausible scenario is that we do have records of time travel but don't know. A time-traveller is much more likely to be treated as a psychiatric patient than as a visitor from the future. If it were just messages, they would need to be in a format where they could be read. Suppose there were signals sent in Morse code. It's not just a matter of someone being able to interpret Morse code, but also a matter of knowing that there is Morse code to be interpreted. Records work because of three things: a known 'ready state' of the material the recording is to take place on, a change that happens to it, and the state after the change that constitutes the record. As we saw in chapter 6, we can only interpret records assuming we at least probably know what the ready state is (i.e. a lower entropy one). But we can also only interpret records if we know what to look for. We need to turn the information in the record into a usable form. On the assumption that time travel is possible, it's entirely possible that there are records of time travel that we haven't been able to recognise or decipher.

Generally, when interpreting events, we should favour the most likely explanation. One of the worries about time travel is that it's such an unlikely explanation that even if it did happen, we might never believe it. In fact, I will pass on some unsolicited life-advice: should a strangely dressed person appear suddenly, and announce that they've come from the future and that they need you to come with them in order to save the future, don't go with them. It's much more likely that this is someone who is lying to you than that they are telling the truth. If they are apparently being chased by another time-traveller, it's much more likely that they are working together than that there are *two* time-travellers. It's also possible that it's a charming and romantic gesture by someone who likes cosplay;

you can go with them if they seem fun. But you shouldn't believe that they are a time-traveller!

Nikk Effingham (2020) defends the view that while time travel is *physically* possible, it is *metaphysically* impossible. So, while physics doesn't rule it out, it is nonetheless impossible. This is a radical view, mainly because physical possibility is normally thought to be those metaphysical possibilities that are also compatible with the laws of physics. The idea that there are things that physics permits but are impossible upends the normal order of things. Whether or not he is right, making sense of time travel as something anyone could actually do is very difficult.

The primary interest in time travel is as a literary device for telling stories in which different contexts collide, or in which we can raise questions about the nature of time, causation, identity, and of how to live in time. It may turn out, then, that the details of time travel don't matter that much if the story is sufficiently good.

QUESTIONS FOR DISCUSSION

1. If you were able to take a bagful of items to the past, when would you go to, and what would you take with you?
2. Does it make sense to say that you *could* kill your grandfather, but you won't? What do 'could' and 'won't' mean in that context?
3. What sort of phenomena would you need to experience for it to be reasonable to conclude time travel to the past had taken place?

NOTES

1 That is, if the pressure differences don't just cause something important to go 'pop' in a deeply unfortunate way.
2 We saw in chapter 7 that the Ancient Stoics thought time was circular.
3 You might also think that time travel can't actually happen. Given some of the stuff that we are supposing to get this situation going, it may be that you just accept the situation is contradictory and stop worrying about it. If time travel is really possible, maybe we should revisit the no contradictions rule?

4 See Lewis 1976 for an influential statement of it.
5 We discussed chaotic systems in chapter 6.
6 'Space-like separated' if you want to use relativistic language.

FURTHER READING

Lewis (1976) is the classic paper on time travel, explaining the distinction between personal time and external time and presenting the grandfather paradox.

Bernstein (2017) presents the idea of a moveable objective present.

Wasserman (2017) gives a book-length discussion of various paradoxes of time travel.

TIME BIAS

Let's turn from considering the nature of time to considering how we live in it. In chapter 7 we considered an affective asymmetry of time: that we have different attitudes towards past and future. It is that difference in attitudes we are interested in now.

We treat other times differently, it seems, depending on whether they are past or future, but also in terms of whether they are nearby or distant. This leads to a series of questions. Most pressingly, *should* we treat other times differently. Later on in the chapter we'll introduce **decision theory** and consider what the costs of changing one's mind are. We'll finish by considering when it is rational to change your mind, in spite of the costs.

NEAR BIAS

When I go shopping, I often find that I select the nearest item to me when picking between a bunch of similar options. Perhaps if I rooted around at the back of the shelf, I'd find a product that was slightly fresher,[1] but I often think it makes very little difference which I select. One tin of rhubarb is much like another. The nearest is usually the most convenient, and the easiest to see. All things being equal, I have a **bias** in favour of the nearest one. Let's call this '*near bias*'. 'Bias', here is being used in the roughly mathematical sense that I'm more likely to do one thing rather than another. In this sense, a roulette wheel can be biased against certain numbers, with no suggestion that it has a personal dislike of them. Even though the Ancient Greeks and Romans thought of Fortune[2] as a goddess who could change your life with a spin of her wheel,

DOI: 10.4324/9781003189459-9

roulette wheels are not persons, they don't decide to land on particular numbers, and they don't like or dislike people.

Suppose my finances are so buoyed up by the sales of this book that I'm giving money to charity.[3] I could give money to a local charity, or one that operates somewhere else in the world. Just as roulette wheels are not people, people are not tins of rhubarb.[4] We might criticize a tendency to only give to charitable causes geographically near to me as a kind of parochialism. The suffering in other parts of the world is as great as it is in my corner of it, and my spending power is often much greater. Given the power of technology, I can send money anywhere in the world almost instantly at very little inconvenience. And given the interconnectedness of the global supply chain, my other economic decisions already impact people elsewhere in the world. My clothes may be made in Bangladesh, and the carbon emissions from my heating system contribute to the rise in sea-levels that threaten the habitability of low-lying parts of Bangladesh.[5] That's before we get into the historical context of the legacies of Empire. Near-bias, in this case, isn't so obviously morally neutral.

Things can be nearby in time as well as nearby in space. Should some embarrassing opinion of mine expressed in my youth emerge, I can dismiss this as being from a long time ago, and when asked about when I plan to retire, I can dismiss that as a long way off yet. The further things are from the present, the less we seem to value them.

We'll come back to some of these issues later on. There are various reasons for being dismissive of past indiscretions, or plans for retirement. I've learnt a lot since I was a callow youth, and there's a huge amount of uncertainty about what the world will be like when I come to retire. These make those times hard to compare to this time. But there are real worries about dismissing events that are distant in time *just because* they are distant.

Suppose you have a week before an important deadline. One course of action is to divide the week into smaller parts of equal size and divide the work into equally sized tasks. You can then evenly distribute those tasks to the different time periods. A second course of action is that you can get the bulk of the work done before the half-way point, and have the last couple of days to relax or deal with any unforeseen problems. A third course of action is that you can wait until the day before, and then try and do it all in one go. This third course of action seems worse than the other two. You don't really get to relax because you are worried about the deadline, right until the deadline. The work is likely to be rushed, and there's no time to deal with unforeseen issues. The third option is one where you procrastinate. Although it is worse, and recognised to be worse, people very often do procrastinate.[6] People doing something they recognise to be worse is puzzling. One explanation for why people do it is that procrastination seems to involve some near bias; it's only when the deadline is near enough to stir you into action that you overcome the resistance to doing the work. If it were uncertainty you were worried by, the second course of action would be vastly preferable, because it means that if something unexpected happens, there's time to adopt a new strategy.

In a series of studies starting in the 1960s led by Walter Mischel,[7] children were given 'the Marshmallow Test'. The test in question is that a small child would be placed in proximity of a tempting treat, like a marshmallow, and told that if it was still there when the experimenter got back they (the child) would be rewarded with an even greater reward (e.g. many marshmallows). The studies found that the ability to 'delay gratification' was an excellent predictor of future academic success and future income. This looks like a test of near bias. Children who can appreciate that they get a greater reward if they wait a short time get greater rewards into adulthood. Near bias, it seems blights lives. This has led people to focus on helping to teach small children 'self-control'. If, like a Stoic sage, they can be immune to temptation, they will have better lives.

Doubts have been raised about this finding by subsequent authors. Part of the explanation will be that children who have grown up in environments where there is a good deal of uncertainty, and people often promise things that don't materialise, have learnt that waiting isn't a sensible option. It's not necessarily self-control or delayed gratification that means that the children don't wait. It's that experience has taught them that a bird in the hand is worth two in the bush; it's better to have a certain reward now than hold out for two uncertain ones later. It might be that children who grow up in stable environments that promote trust are more likely to have better lives. Or it could be that self-control and a stable, trusting environment are both important. In general, though, there is a consensus that near bias *based purely on distance in time* is something to be avoided. It's harder to work out which real-life situations are pure in that way.

PAST BIAS

It's not just bias against things at some temporal distance that we might be concerned by, but also the tendency to want bad things to be in the past and good things to be in the future.

Derek Parfit (1984:165–6) is responsible for the thought experiment that gets much contemporary thinking about past bias going. It's quite a complicated thought experiment, so I shall quote it in full:

> I am in some hospital, to have some kind of surgery. Since this is completely safe, and always successful, I have no fears about the effects. The surgery may be brief, or it may instead take a long time. Because I have to cooperate with the surgeon, I cannot have anaesthetics. I have had this surgery once before, and I can remember how painful it is. Under a new policy, because the operation is so painful, patients are now afterwards made to forget it. Some drug removes their memories of the last few hours. I have just woken up. I cannot remember going to sleep. I ask my nurse if it has been decided when my operation is to be, and how long it must take. She says she knows the facts about me and another patient, but that she cannot remember which facts apply to whom. She can tell me only that the following is true. I may be the patient who had his operation yesterday. In that case, my operation was the longest ever performed, lasting ten hours. I may instead be the patient who is to have a short operation today. It is either true that I did suffer for ten hours, or true that I shall suffer for one hour. I ask the nurse to find out which is true. While she is away, it is clear to me which I prefer to be true. If I learn that the first is true I shall be greatly relieved.

This thought experiment is meant to get you thinking about a broadly realistic case where you have a preference for whether something is in the past or in the future. You don't get to *decide* which, but you have views about which one you would like it to be. There are a few features of the experiment that it's important to notice:

- It compares future pain with past pain.
- The pains are meant to be similar enough that it's plausible that more pain is worse than less pain.
- Uncertainty and future painful memories are supposed to be irrelevant in the example.

If you would prefer pain to be in the past, that suggests that you have an asymmetry of value. Past pain is better than future pain. Similarly, you might think future pleasure is better than past pleasure. These are biases in favour of the past or future that are distinct from near bias. It's not a matter of how distant from you the things are, but in which direction.

It's less clear that past bias is bad in the way near bias is. After all, in chapter 6 we considered various ways in which the past is different to the future. Just as with near bias, the idea is that past bias is meant to be a bias that is left over *after we've taken account* of the factors involving uncertainty, differences in context, etc.

'Time bias' is the term I'm using to cover near bias in the case of time, and past/future bias. You could say time bias is having systematic preferences about when events take place. There's a live debate about whether time bias (once we've taken other factors into account) is bad. In general, economists think time bias is fine as long as it's consistent, and philosophers think that time bias is a bad thing. Some of us might think that it's difficult to find examples of time bias where other factors are not involved, but it is those other factors that justify the bias, and not location in time by itself.

In the next section we'll introduce some mathematical apparatus for thinking about decisions. It's not going to be very difficult maths, but it's worth understanding the basic principles, because public policy decisions that affect you are made using these techniques. Indeed, one of the places that time bias really matters is in responses to climate change. If future generations are distant in time, and we don't care about their needs as much as we do with present concerns, we are likely to come up with policies that procrastinate about preventing climate change or preparing for it.

DECISION THEORY

Decision theory is the theory of what makes decisions *rational*. That is, it is the theory of when decisions are good ones in a minimal sense that they aren't self-defeating, inconsistent, or contradictory. It is *not* the theory of how to make decisions.[8] It is neutral about what makes decisions ethically good. It can be really useful for showing that some decisions are guaranteed to leave you worse off. One of the things decision theory says is that you shouldn't choose courses of action that are guaranteed to leave you worse off. You might think that something so obvious doesn't need stating. Alternatively, you might think the problem is that if people are taking bad decisions, they often aren't interested in people pointing out that the decision is not merely risky but guaranteed to leave them worse off. But you nonetheless might find it comforting to be able to articulate to yourself what they did wrong.

The central idea of decision theory is that you have a *decision problem* in which you chose amongst some outcomes. These outcomes might have different values attached to them. They also might have different likelihoods of happening. So, if you bet on a coin toss, for example, you can bet that the coin will land heads. In this situation, you win on heads and lose on tails. If you don't bet, you get to keep your money regardless of whether the coin lands heads or tails (in fact, if you don't bet, they probably won't bother tossing the coin).

In a decision problem, you weigh up how good an outcome would be if it goes well, how bad it would be if it goes badly, and how likely those outcomes are. By weighting the values by the likelihoods, you get a number. Let's call this number the '**expected utility**'. It's how much value ('utility') you expect, on average, to get. You then compare that outcome to the others, and work out which outcome has the highest expected utility (i.e. 'maximises' expected utility). Decision theory is going to recommend the outcome that maximises expected utility.

But expected utility doesn't always take into account your level of 'risk aversion'. Risk aversion is where, all things being equal, you prefer a situation with less risk, even if the expected reward is the same. If you are 'risk-seeking' then, all things being equal, you prefer a situation with more risk, even if the expected reward is the same. If you really dislike risk, doing something that on average leaves you better off but risks leaving you much worse off might not be worth it. Playing Russian Roulette – where 5/6 of the time you win life-transformingly BIG and 1/6 of the time you shoot yourself in the head – might not be worth it, because although winning BIG would be really amazing, avoiding losing might be a sensible choice.

If you had the option of playing a different version of the game, where you win BIG 5/6 of the time, and the other 1/6 of the time neither win nor lose anything, it would be better to play than not to play. 'Better off' here means that whatever stuff you value, you will have more of that than you had before. With this modified Russian Roulette, you are either in a better position than you started out, or now in a worse position. Situations that leave you either better off or no worse off are said to **dominate** the other situations. If an option dominates another option, it is *irrational* to take the dominated option. Lots of decision theory is concerned with working out which options dominate other options. It's a helpful way of narrowing down the options you need to consider. If one option dominates another option, you don't need to deliberate about the dominated option and can remove it from consideration.

There are some options – strongly dominant ones – that are guaranteed to leave you better off. But there are also actions that are guaranteed to leave you worse off. Indeed, there can be sequences of decisions, where, at each point in the sequence you do the thing that maximises expected utility for that decision problem, but *as a sequence* leaves you worse off than you would have been. So you are doing the best thing at each step in the sequence (not the dominated thing), but the whole sequence is dominated by another sequence. These sequences are particularly important to us, because we're going to get an argument that time bias leaves us in a position where we are always open to being tempted into such a sequence of actions.

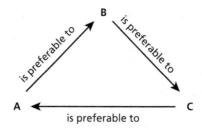

Figure 8.1 Intransitive preferences

Let's start with a case where you have 'intransitive preferences'. So, for example, you are choosing between three options: A, B and C (see Figure 8.1):

You value A more than B, B more than C, and C more than A.

Suppose you currently have C, and I offer you B (for a small consideration). You accept; after all you prefer B to C.

You have B. I offer you A (for a further small fee). You accept, after all, you prefer A to B.

You have A. I offer you C (for a further small fee). You accept, right? After all, you prefer C to A.

Each decision has given you what you want, in exchange for a small fee. Provided the value of the fee is less than the difference in value between the two options, it makes sense for you to change. But because the preferences are intransitive – they don't obey the rule that if A is better than B, and B is better than C, A must be better than C – I can keep persuading you to change options, and keep getting a small fee out of you. This situation is known as a **money pump**.[9]

The worry about time bias is that it opens you up to a money pump, or something similar. It needn't be money, but could be pain, or effort, or feet of liquorice. The point is that if your values form a certain kind of structure, you are open to exploitation.[10] As we are about to see, time bias leaves you open to money pump style structures.

FUTURE DISCOUNTING

Now we have a brief sketch of some key concepts in decision theory, we can talk about time bias in more detail. We tend to treat the distant future as mattering less than the immediate future, as we have seen. And we tend to prefer painful things to be in the past and pleasurable things to be in the future. These tendencies can be given value in decision theory. We can speak of a **discount function** that specifies the amount by which we count future events as mattering less (i.e. *discount* them). Discounting future pleasure is one explanation of what is going on when children eat the marshmallow in the Marshmallow Test; two marshmallows later is considered to be worth less than one now. (Though it might not be valuing the marshmallows that explains the result, but self-control, or uncertainty, or trust etc.)

Valuing future times less than present ones is a problem, because our discount function may lead to us changing our minds. Imagine you tend to prefer the larger reward later to the smaller reward sooner. You are consistent in this, until the smaller reward gets sufficiently close. Then you prefer the smaller reward sooner. Then the smaller reward is in the past, and you discount the past too. Now you wish the reward were in the future, and would swap the small reward in the past for the larger one still to come, if only you could. This looks like a recipe for regret.

This is a 'preference reversal'. It's two, in fact. You have gone from wanting the larger reward later to the smaller reward sooner (reversal 1 at t_1), and then back to wanting the larger reward later (reversal 2 at t_2) (See Figure 8.2). Reversal 1 is due to near bias and reversal 2 is due to past bias.

Time bias means that most people don't start saving for retirement as early as they might because a little money now is felt to be much better than a lot more in several decades. In fact, this sort of future discounting isn't just something that individual people do out of temptation or weakness. It is routine for companies to discount future prices by a 'corporate discount rate', meaning that long term effects of decisions don't count for as much as shorter term effects. Attempts to mitigate climate change are not 'financially viable' because the financial benefits of having a habitable planet in 100 years are discounted so much that it's better to make a profit now.[11]

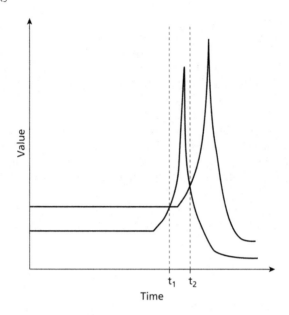

Figure 8.2 Preferences over time

Frank Ramsey (1928:543) was quite forceful in his condemnation of such future discounting in public policy. He said it was 'ethically indefensible and arises merely from the weakness of the imagination'.

One response might be that future discounting is fine, provided it is the right kind of discounting. If our future discounting is:

- At a constant rate
- Independent of what stuff we're valuing
- Independent of what kind of outcome we get

we avoid such preference reversals. Let's call this *exponential* discounting.

Note that exponential discounting isn't what people or other animals naturally do, but it is a form of discounting that avoids preference reversals. But this doesn't settle the question of what rate that should be, and it doesn't resolve the problem that significant events in the far future might be treated like they don't matter until they become near problems. Exponential discounting still involves near bias, but because it is constant, consistent near bias, it doesn't lead to preference reversals.

TEMPORAL NEUTRALITY

Preston Greene and Meghan Sullivan (2015) argue that we should avoid both past bias and near bias. We should be neutral about when things happen. Technically, this is a special case of exponential discounting. On *temporal neutrality* we discount at a constant rate of zero.

Their argument is that we don't need to discount for time in addition to uncertainty and other relevant factors. There's nothing about the location of events in time that means we should value them differently on the basis of those locations.

Temporal neutrality is a radical position. It's standard in the social sciences and in business to assume some exponential discount rate. But temporal neutrality is popular amongst defenders of a particular ethical approach: utilitarianism.

LONGTERMISM

Utilitarianism is the view, first defended by Francis Hutcheson, that '*that action* is *best*, which procures the *greatest happiness* for the *greatest numbers*; and that *worst*, which, in *like manner*, occasions *misery*'.[12] This view measures actions by their outcomes. On some versions it measures outcomes in terms of pleasure and pain, and on others in terms of a richer set of values. But every person counts the same, regardless of what country they are in, or whether they are enemy or ally.

For many contemporary utilitarians, it is a straightforward extension of this view that future people count as much as present ones. Derek Parfit, who came up with the thought experiment we discussed in the section on 'Past bias', thought that we should consider merely possible future people in our calculations too. So policies to fight climate change by reducing the number of people who are born can be objected to because they are bad for the people who would otherwise get born but don't.[13] By similar reasoning, the destruction of habitats for wildlife can be justified, some claim, because the future lives of the animals who live in those habitats would be 'worse than nothing on average' given all the pain that they would experience living in the wild.[14]

The connection with the discussion of existence and actuality in chapter 7 is important here. Whether the merely possible future is out there somewhere, or whether it lacks existence/actuality might make a difference to what sort of policies we adopt when it comes to issues involving potential future people/animals.

'Longtermism', as it's known, is the view that we should take decisions based on their long-term consequences, rather than prioritising their immediate consequences. And 'long-term' here means scales in the tens of thousands of years. But one key objection to longtermism is that it doesn't really recommend anything.[15] The defence of temporal neutrality above was always that we shouldn't discount for *location in time*, but allowed for discounting for uncertainty and other relevant factors. On the scales that longtermists are interested in, uncertainty is a pretty huge factor. In fact, for reasons we will consider later, it's just not clear that we can make sense of how to value things in 10,000 years time. If we think 10,000 years in the past, that was around the time of the invention of agriculture. Making sense of life and culture across those kind of time spans is exceptionally difficult when we have access to the archaeological record of that time. It is far more likely that civilisation in 10,000 years time will be almost totally unrecognisable to us than that it will be easily understood by those making policy now.

PREFERENCE REVERSALS

Having laid out the issues of temporal discounting, let's turn to preference reversals. We've established that they open you up to exploitation. But are they always bad?

Preference reversals can be understood in terms of failures of 'consistency'. Consistency fails when one of two conditions are met. Either the assumption called '*stationarity*' doesn't hold, or the assumption called '*invariance*' doesn't hold. I'll explain what these two mean.

STATIONARITY

If a decision-maker values outcomes just on the basis of how good/bad they are and the amount of time between them, they are 'stationary'. This is what the exponential discounter satisfies that other future discounters don't. A delay of a week makes the same difference regardless of what week it is. If you have two options; a trip to Bristol tomorrow and a trip to Bristol in six months, you are stationary if it would make no difference to the decision problem if we delayed both potential trips by a week. So if you preferred to go to Bristol tomorrow rather than in six months, you should still prefer to go to Bristol in a week, rather than in six months and a week. If a delay of a week makes a difference, it makes the same difference to both options when stationarity is satisfied.

INVARIANCE

Invariance isn't about delay, but about what time you are asked to express a preference. Suppose you are planning to go to Bristol in a week. If you are 'invariant', how much you value going to Bristol should be the same now as it is in a week's time, when you are in Bristol. There's nothing special about a particular time.[16]

Whereas stationarity compared your preferences about two different outcomes at one time, invariance compares your preferences about one outcome at two different times. If two out of consistency, stationarity and invariance are true, the third must be true. If two are false, the third must be false.

As soon as you start using realistic examples, it becomes clear that we violate at least one of those quite frequently. If I'm invited to visit Bristol tomorrow, turning up a week later, when my host is visiting someone else, is no good. But if I'm planning to visit in six months, my host may not have any preference which week I come, since it doesn't interfere with their other plans. Once I make plans with my host, I'm open to exploitation. Oh no!

Similarly, when I get to Bristol, I may be disappointed. It may be that for reasons of weather, or health, or *force majeure*, the trip isn't as fun as I had hoped. How much I value being in Bristol might be different once I am there compared to the value I put on the trip in prospect. I've reversed my preferences. Oh no!

But the point about these realistic examples is that it's not *location in time* that makes the difference; it's something else. It's true I'm open to exploitation, but it isn't through *irrationality* but because something relevant has changed.

CHANGING YOUR MIND

There are many reasons that you might change your mind about what's valuable and how likely it is. Let's run through some.

CHANGES OF INFORMATION

Information is a key reason it is rational to change your mind. When criticised for frequently changing his mind, the economist John Maynard Keynes is reported to have said: 'When my information changes, I alter my conclusions. What do you do, sir?'

Indeed, the need to change decisions in light of new information is often appealed to in policy debates. Lord Lisvane, in a speech in the UK House of Lords, used the following analogy:

> It is as though I have three elderly and extremely nervous aunts of whom I am very fond. I decide to give them a treat and ask them to discuss what they would like to do. They have a discussion and arrive at a democratic solution, which is that they would like to go to the cinema tomorrow. I look in the local paper and discover that the only films on offer are "Reservoir Dogs" and "The Texas Chainsaw Massacre". What am I going to say to my highly nervous—indeed, squeamish—but much-loved aunts: "You must stick with your democratic decision"? Or do I say, "Now you know what's on offer, what do you think?"[17]

When there is a change of information, it is often rational to change one's mind, even though that will come with some costs. It might mean that under conditions of uncertainty, it's a bad idea to pay significant costs to commit to a particular course of action, but sometimes, such costs will be unavoidable.

CHANGE OF CIRCUMSTANCES

It might not just be information that changes. If you were planning to visit a friend and then you have an argument with them, it is not just the *information* that you had an argument that might provoke you to change your mind, but the argument itself. You may no longer want to see them or they may no longer want to see you. The outbreak of war, fire, flood or famine may change your priorities. And this seems totally reasonable. If these circumstances were predictable, you perhaps ought to have planned for them, but if you find you have an infectious disease for example, or that you now risk death by attempting to leave the house, it is rational to change your social plans.

CHANGES IN WHAT'S ACTUAL

It might be that the difference between what's potential and what's actual is significant. Elizabeth Harman (2009) has an example of a woman who had a child as a teenager. She can compare the life she actually has to the life that she could have had had she waited to have a child. There are various ways that life could have been different: how happy she was, how financially secure she was, how good a mother she was, how happy the child that she would have had would have been. She admits that her life would have been better in every way that matters if she had waited to have a child. The potential child would, on average, have been happier than the actual child was. Nonetheless, she wouldn't change the child she has for another one.

The thought here is that the actual child matters not just in terms of how it scores on a bunch of measures of value, but it matters just being that child. It is *that* actual child the mother loves, and not some potential other child. When you are choosing amongst potential options, you can trade them off against each other. You can swap them for one another based on their properties, much as you can swap tins of rhubarb for each other based on their qualities. But actual children are not like tins of rhubarb. One way of putting this is that actual people are not *fungible*. They have different identities that matter for the purposes of making decisions. From the perspective of policy makers, decisions may often abstract from the particular actualities of the individuals. But parents, siblings, friends and loved ones may not.

If the passage of time is a change from potential to actual, this will mean that there is a really important difference between past and future in terms of value. This difference might explain why we don't have to consider the loss of life of merely potential future people the way we should for actual present people. Once again, we can see that some of the theoretical debate about change and the arrow of time is interacting with the ethical debate about how we make decisions. As Setiya (2014) suggests, certain kinds of moral relationships, (such as loving ones) depend on co-existence.

CHANGES IN YOUR VALUES

It's not just your information and circumstances that can change. It's not just what exists/is actual that can change. *You* can change![18]

Some experiences change your relationship to the world. Having a child doesn't just change things for the child, but usually also for the parent. Many other experiences (traveling, falling in love, studying philosophy, changing jobs, etc.) can change who you are in important ways. For one thing, they can change what you can imagine. Having new experiences means that you can imagine different things and make decisions between options that you couldn't understand before. But also, new experiences can change what sorts of things you care about. L.A. Paul (2015) calls these 'transformative experiences'.

You can also undergo transformative experiences. That is, you can change what you value (what your preferences are). This might be a result of a profound experience that changes what matters to you. Transformative experiences are a challenge for decision theory. Because the original idea is that you work out what you value and how likely it is, and then choose the option that maximises expected utility. Or at the very least, choose an option that isn't dominated by another option.

Transformative experiences are a challenge, because it's the criteria that decide whether or not you think a decision *counts* as good that change. Suppose that when you are young, you want to live the bohemian life of an artist, and are prepared to put up with no money, and poor living conditions to be surrounded by exciting and interesting people who make art and music and talk about ideas. You suspect that when you are older you will care about comfortable beds, and interest rates, and job security (and stability and predictability). From the point of view of the older you, saving towards a pension, getting skills that make you more employable, and not doing things with bad long-term health risks looks like it is the best course. But from the point of view of you as a younger person, following your passion, taking risks, and having adventures seems like the best course. But how do we weigh up these perspectives; they are both your perspectives! But because of the profound changes in values you have undergone, you can't really relate to each other. In chapter 10 we'll think through the problems of living a life involving these sorts of changes. For now, let's leave it as a category of reasons where it is acceptable to change your preferences.

One final thought about these reasons to change your mind. These are all reasons distinct from location or distance in time. They don't represent time bias as we've been discussing it. But we might worry about the extent to which we can separate considerations of temporal discounting from these various changes that take place as time passes. Callender (2021) argues that we can't separate out pure temporal considerations from impure ones that involve these factors. Perhaps we can in principle, but when criticising people for irrationality when they are inconsistent, we would need to be quite confident that none of these factors are relevant. It's just not clear that we can do that, Callender argues.

To sum up, most humans are biased in favour of the near and treat the past and future differently. There are questions about whether this is rational, and what kind of discounting we should engage in. What initially seemed straightforward (do what maximises expected utility) has left important questions unanswered about how much we should value the future and the past.

QUESTIONS FOR DISCUSSION

1. What's bad about having intransitive preferences? Is merely being *open* to exploitation concerning?
2. In practice, is it possible to separate pure time bias from those situations that involve other reasons for changing one's mind?
3. Is it rational to discount the future (even if one does so consistently)?

NOTES

1 Good stock rotation dictates putting the new stock at the back,
2 *Tyche* in Greek, and *Fortuna* in Latin.
3 Lol
4 A surprising amount of philosophy involves keeping differences like this clear.
5 2/3 of Bangladesh is less than 5m above sea-level.
6 Including me.

7 E.g. Mischel, Shoda and Rodriguez (1989).

8 I know of a group of academics that used to have a weekly meeting in which they would read and discuss the latest research in decision theory. They stopped meeting because they couldn't decide when to meet.

9 Davidson, McKinsey and Suppes (1955)

10 It's not that you are guaranteed to be exploited, because you could have a rule where you only change your mind once and then stick to your decision, no matter what it is. But simply finding yourself in such a structure is a sign that things have gone wrong.

11 See e.g. Knoke, Gosling and Paul (2020).

12 Cited in Raphael (1969:284), emphasis original.

13 See Parfit (1984) on 'The Repugnant Conclusion'.

14 MacAskill (2022:213)

15 See Lenman (2000).

16 Claims that Christmas is 'the most wonderful time of the year' are therefore incompatible with invariance.

17 Lisvane (2018)

18 I believe in you! You can do it!

FURTHER READING

Sullivan (2018) provides a book length argument that it is irrational to have any time bias.

Pettigrew (2018) discusses the problems transformative experiences create for decision theory.

Callender (2021) argues that the arguments of consistency over time have failed to reckon with the difficulty of separating pure time bias from other considerations.

9

REWRITING HISTORY

In the previous chapter we became interested in how we think about different times in the context of decision making. However, we aren't just interested in making decisions, but also in understanding. In fact, you might think that if we are to make good decisions, we must first understand the past. This chapter deals with some issues with our attempt to understand the past through the study of history.

REWRITING HISTORY AND CHANGING THE PAST

Back in chapter 7 we thought about the arrow of time, and the idea that there is an asymmetry of intervention. You can sometimes do something about the future, but you can't change the past. Speaking to historians, one quickly discovers that they spend a lot of their time not simply finding things out about the past, but redescribing it. The study of history is not a steady accumulation of knowledge, but a constant revision of how we think about the past.

There are cases in which the facts about what happened at a particular time seem to change from what they were at that time. This sounds a little like you *can* intervene on the past. That impression is misleading, as we shall see, but it's important to acknowledge that it sometimes looks like we can change the past.

One example of this is when two people begin a relationship. Imagine someone invites their new acquaintance for a coffee, so they can get to know each other. For all anyone knows at the time, this encounter could go a number of different ways. Suppose that they have a nice conversation, and then, after the chat, silently come to the conclusion that cordial acquaintances is all they are likely to be to

DOI: 10.4324/9781003189459-10

each other. Upon describing the event later, it will be very easy for either party to say 'that wasn't a date, we just had a coffee and a chat!' No-one suggested at any time during the event that it was a date, even if there was some initial attraction between the two people.

Suppose instead that they spark, and arrange another meeting, and then another, soon leading to an ongoing romantic relationship. Someone later asks them 'when did you guys start dating?' and they might refer back to that chat over coffee as the first date.

Ostensibly, the very same meeting over coffee is, in one future scenario, very definitely not the kind of romantic encounter known as a 'date', and in the other scenario was a hugely significant romantic encounter; the first date in a long relationship. In fact, we can think of cases where whether or not something is a date is only settled afterwards, by whether a subsequent meeting takes place. Without changing the contents of the cups, the location, or the words that are exchanged, the very same event can have very different properties, based on what happens later. What's more, in issuing the initial invitation, neither party may know, or have even entertained, the significance of the event. Almost any event, including your reading this *right now*, could come to have a significance you haven't anticipated in light of future events, even when this very event is long past. Arthur Danto (1985:340) remarks:

> In effect, so far as the future is open, the past is so as well; and insofar as we cannot tell what events will someday be seen as connected with the past, the past is always going to be differently described.

It is this feature that makes history particularly interesting to a philosopher of time, because the idea that the past is settled and the future open stands in contrast to the endless possibilities for reinterpreting the historical course of events. This reinterpretation *matters*. That's because we use history to make sense of what's taking place now and what might take place in the future.

As James Baldwin (1966:174) put it:

> History, as nearly no one seems to know, is not merely something to be read. And it does not refer merely, or even principally, to the past. On the contrary, the great force of history comes from the fact that we carry it within us, are unconsciously controlled by it in many

ways, and history is literally present in all that we do. It could scarcely be otherwise, since it is to history that we owe our frames of reference, our identities, and our aspirations.

One of the reasons for engaging in history is political. It is useful to have some shared interpretations of the world we live in through which to collectively interpret our lives, plans, and decisions. History is useful, as Baldwin says, for providing shared frames of reference. Indeed, precisely because it is useful for these purposes, it is also dangerous, because those shared forms of interpretation can come to take hold and become untethered from reality. If *all* that mattered were shared frames of reference, the most useful ones would do. But one reason to care about *history*, rather than for example, national myths, is that history is meant to confront us with the inconvenience of the past. One of the respects in which we are stuck with the past is that it is often more complicated and less convenient than we would like it to be.

In this chapter we will discuss the relationship between the endlessly rewritable history and the past we are stuck with. We'll think about the stories we tell about history, and then we'll think about the constraint that being *accurate* places on history.

HISTORY AND THE PAST

We can reconcile the claim that we can't change the past but are constantly revising history by making a distinction. 'The past' is just the stuff earlier than now: the sequence of objects, processes and their properties in their locations at various times. The past is what it is whether we know about it, and regardless of what we think about it. It is how it is, and cannot be changed, except by changing its relation to later things. 'History' is a description of the past (or the project of providing that description).[1] The descriptions can change without changing the stuff earlier than now. There's very little to say about the stuff earlier than now that is not history, because as soon as you say things about it, you are dealing with the stuff earlier than now under particular descriptions. We can't just talk about the stuff without choosing particular perspectives and relations to the future that frame such talk.

History is a **hermeneutic** discipline, because it deals with inter-pretation. Indeed, it is *doubly hermeneutic*, since it tends to deal with written records of history, so historians are interpreting someone's past interpretation of the past. This means that we need to make sense of how to interpret the past interpretations, and how to relate those past interpretations to the past.

One very basic form of history is *the chronicle*. This is just a list of what happened when. Even this involves interpretation, since deci-sions have been taken about what is worth recording and to whom. Let's take as an example an excerpt from **The Annals of St Gall**:

709 Hard Winter. Duke Gottfried died
710 Hard year and deficient in crops
711
712 Flood Everywhere
713
714 Pippin, mayor of the palace died

The number on the left is the year, and the description says what happened in that year. Note that it is concerned with 'natu-ral' events (the winter, crop yields, floods) as well as the deaths of important people. The historian Hayden White (1980:6) argued that even with this very limited description, we still learn a lot about the concerns of the people writing the chronicle of this period.

We might think that there is more to history than giving us a sequence of significant events, as the chronicle does. We might think that history allows us to *explain* those events, perhaps by using a narrative form. The historian can use stories to make the past understandable, and to show how distinct events might be con-nected, both to each other and to our present concerns. White, amongst others, argues for the importance of narrative explanations to history.[2]

NARRATIVE

'Narrative' is a technical term for story-telling. Usually, narra-tives have an author (this may be individual or a collective author), and an intended audience (which may differ from the actual audience). Narratives have a number of features that make them interesting:

- A narrative invites the reader to adopt a temporal perspective of that narrated.
- The temporal perspective of the audience may differ from that narrated.
- There is some authorial evaluation of what is being narrated.
- The narration has unity, and often a sense of closure.
- Narrative has central and peripheral characters.

When we tell stories, we usually have some, at least minimal, *world-building*, in which we are invited to imagine being immersed in a situation which is not actually happening to us at present. Indeed, we can treat past or future times as if they were present. We can imagine rather alien situations which are neither past nor future to us, but entirely fictional worlds.

When we tell stories, we usually go beyond giving a mere chronicle in which we list facts in an order. But even in the case of a chronicle, there is some evaluation going on. In some stories this can be rather unsubtle. If you are describing the reign of William I of England with the description 'William the Conqueror' or alternatively 'William the Bastard', you are saying something about your attitude. Children's stories often feature the good king, the wicked queen, the humble peasant etc. and don't really invite us to make up our minds about where our own sympathies lie. Such editorialising is rightly considered biased history.[3] But *some* evaluation is inevitable. Consider, once more, the Annals of St Gall. Why is the mayor's death worth remarking on? Why are floods bad? A narrative involves a story-teller making decisions about what to include and what to leave out.

Stories inevitably involve evaluation, because they inevitably involve some attempt at finding a unity that allows the story to be recognizable as having a plot. The story has to start somewhere, and finish somewhere. It has to have something that allows it to hang together as a single story, whether that's a unity of theme, of location, or time, or because it follows some particular individual or group. Perhaps it has all of these. Inevitably, it will involve presenting something as a foreground against a background. Although there are likely to be narratives in palaeontology and geology, in the history of human affairs, we are likely to be concerned with actions, and so with the actors who carried them out. So just as stories generally involve selecting something to be fore-grounded against a background, stories about humans involve characters (either individuals or groups) to foreground as the protagonists of the story against the background of other characters and events.

The 1994 Peter Segal film *Naked Gun 33⅓* has a scene in which joke historical narratives have been sensationalised into award-nominated movies, such as 'Fatal Affair: One woman's ordeal to overcome the death of her cat. Set against the background of the Hindenberg disaster'.[4] The joke lies in the absurd inappropriateness of the evaluative judgements in choosing to foreground the death of a pet against a more significant and more tragic event. The invisibility of the evaluative foregrounding we get in narratives that attempt to avoid bias is a sign that they are widely shared (perhaps for good reason), not that they are 'value free'.

We might think of narratives as allowing us to explain sequences of events in a certain way. Whereas causal explanation might get us to explain later events as effects of earlier ones, narratives allow us to make sense of earlier times in terms of later ones. We can think of an event as leading to something, or going somewhere, or culminating in a comprehensible conclusion. Not all stories have satisfying resolutions, but there's no doubt that we tend to find stories that do 'go somewhere' much more satisfying. This contrast with whether we are interested in causal explanations or narrative explanations is a continuing divide in history, where 'scientific' approaches such as sociological and economic history tend to focus on causes of events rather than using narratives to make sense of them. Even causal explanations tend to involve some narrative elements as to why 'the events' are presented in this way, and which features of the causal network are important for explanation.

One of the most crucial features of narratives is that they have specific structures. What kind of narrative something is can be changed, just by adding an extra bit of the story. Jane Austen's novels are narratives that usually end in a wedding, but *Pride and Prejudice* would be a very different story if we added a chapter to the end detailing the acrimonious divorce of the D'Arcys. That it has a happy ending is essential to the narrative that it is, and our interpretation of the earliest chapters is shaped by the fact that they lead to the conclusion they do. Historical narratives are much like fictional ones, except that we appear to have an additional constraint that they are *accurate*.

I have spoken, so far, as though narratives are stories that start at the beginning, and move in a straightforward way through a sequence of unfolding events, until we get to the end. But narratives need not have a linear structure. In literature we often encounter story-telling techniques involving flash-backs, flash-forwards, etc. 'Retconning' – retroactive changes to allow for story continuity – is a particularly interesting technique, where events previously established to have happened are explained away. The TV show Dallas became infamous in the mid-1980s by following its 9th series by showing that everything in the 9th series had been a dream of one of the characters (Pamela Ewing) in the opening episode of the 10th series.

Historians can also make use of such devices in their narratives. Indeed, authoritarian regimes have regularly been known to change history textbooks to remove or distort embarrassing past episodes. Revision to history needn't be as part of a cover-up, however. The so-called 'Glorious Revolution' of 1688 where William of Orange invaded England might only be considered glorious from a certain political point of view. While it was a bloodless revolution in England, it was rather bloodier in Ireland, for example. Appreciating that the historical narrative has excluded (perhaps systematically) certain perspectives might be a reason for re-examining and reassessing the histories we tell.

Indeed, rather than thinking of time as linear, or branching like a tree, French philosophers Deleuze and Guattari use the idea of a '*rhizome*'. Rhizomes, such as strawberry plants, are plants that send roots out, and rather than going down into the soil, those roots go sideways and then form new sprouts elsewhere. The idea is, roughly, that in making sense of time we are always beginning in the middle and making connections with things both in the past and in the imagined future: 'A rhizome has no beginning or end; it is always in the middle, between things, interbeing, *intermezzo*' (Deleuze and Guattari, 1980/2004: 25).

Even if the passage of time, discussed in the first part of the book, is a linear change from potential to actual, from future to past, our interpretation of time is always caught in between future and past, stretching out in both directions. We can only make sense of the past because of the ways we are able to imagine the future developing. We are only able to imagine the future because of the history with which we approach it. We only endure present discomfort for distant goals over present comfort because of what will have been.

Which events in the past count as *significant*, and get to be included in our history depends on how we understand our present situation and what future we are trying to bring about. What objects and processes characterise our current situation depends on what we have previously recognised as significant, and the futures we imagine are projections of our current situation, charactered in that particular way, into different future possibilities. As we go through different circumstances (such as the transformative experiences discussed in chapter 8, perhaps), we might have to re-imagine the entire narrative as we come to imagine different futures, and describe ourselves as the product of different pasts, and highlight different events or characters as the foreground around which we unify the story.

We will come back, towards the end of the chapter, to questions about the objectivity, reality, or accuracy of historians' narratives. Even if historians often make use of narratives, and narratives have philosophically interesting features, the *differences* between literary fiction and historical narrative are important. For all I have said so far, it could be that the narratives are entirely imposed on the past by the authors, or found within the past, *waiting to be told*. There is no reason to think that the past is only compatible with a single narrative, and we haven't considered issues of how to deal with competing narratives. Before we move on to such issues, I want to think a little more about the techniques that historical narratives may involve.

EMPLOTMENT

If history imposes a narrative on the past, what kind of narrative is it? A tempting view is that there are a limited number of basic plots that stories have. So we find sequences of historical events, with historical figures to bring into the foreground in order to fit those plots. Hayden White (1980) considers four such basic plots: The

Romantic, the Tragic, the Comic and Satirical. I don't see why there should be a limited number of plots, and in any case other plots would need to be included.[5]

The plots:

- Romantic
  - A hero overcomes obstacles in their path in the process transforming both themselves and the world.
- Tragic
  - Some initial division inevitably leads to disastrous consequences (and maybe death), with some redemption perhaps for those who learn from it.
- Comic
  - The Comic begins with division, but ends non-transformatively, with things being resolved, but the world roughly as it was before.
- Satirical
  - The Satirical begins with division, but belief in change is just hubris. The characters are trapped in their circumstances, and no progress gets made.

These four 'emplotments' involve a similar basic narrative structure. There's some unsatisfactory situation, and something happens in an attempt to change it. As you can see, the Romantic and Tragic plots involve a significant change (perhaps a transformative experience). The Comic and the Satiric don't involve any transformation, merely a temporary departure from the norm. The Heroic and the Comic have happy endings, whereas the Tragic and the Satiric don't.

We can certainly see the temptation to provide stories with clear heroes, or villains, with the good ending happily and the bad unhappily; such narratives structures are very satisfying. They save us a good deal of work, for one thing. Once we know what structure we are dealing with, we very quickly know how to make sense of the narrative we are given.

One of the dangers of such narrative forms is that they are so satisfying that it can be easy to twist the facts to fit the demands of the plot. We find ourselves attempting to decide whether Winston Churchill was the heroic British Prime Minister who led the country to victory in World War Two, or the villainous imperialist who oversaw the Bengal famine. The temptation is to think that one of these stories, unlike the other, *gets things right*. But, of course, we needn't choose just one such story. Most people are many things and can contribute to many narratives. This is a theme that we will pick up in the next chapter.

LAWS, INTENTIONS, STORIES

One case that can be made for the significance of narrative to history is the role in explaining human actions. A distinctive thing about history is that it tends to involve one-off events. Explaining the causes of the Crimean War (1853-1856) in terms of law-like generalisations doesn't get very far. We can appeal to the strategic location of Crimea, and European concerns about Russian Expansionism, that might apply to many times, but explaining that particular conflict is likely to involve factors that just wouldn't make sense at other time periods or other places. We can come up with risk-factors for particular types of event. But even if there were social laws, it would be very difficult to work out how to use them in practice. They would be exceptionally sensitive to small changes in circumstances. History is often concerned with what *might easily* have happened, rather than what *must* have happened.

Rather than appeal to laws, we might appeal, instead, to psychological explanations. R.G. Collingwood, one of the most influential philosophers of history, and also a practicing archaeologist, had the idea that, unlike the natural sciences, history was concerned with understanding the reasons for which people did things. The aim of history, according to Collingwood, is to 're-enact' the past.[6]

This is not to suggest that Collingwood was advocating Live-Action Role Play ('LARPing') as the primary means of conducting historical studies, but that the aim of history is to be able to make sense of a person's decisions in terms of their presuppositions and reasons for acting. The idea is that we make sense of the assumptions by which they operated, what would have appeared valuable from their point of view, and to *rationally reconstruct* the reasoning that they could have appealed to.

Collingwood's approach places human actions and intentions at the centre of history, rather than trying to explain things in terms of causal laws. Collingwood was influential, partly because he emphasised that history was a hermeneutic enterprise. Unlike the sciences, the goal is interpretation, rather than causal explanation. But we might hesitate to say that the dividing line between historical and scientific explanations is always very sharp. When we describe the social world, interpretation matters, but so too do facts about biology, maths, and physics.

If technological developments change what it is possible to achieve, this might change the ways society is structured and consequently the social forces that shape significant events. Explaining how the invention of the printing press made possible the spread of the scientific and philosophical ideas which ultimately led to the French Revolution might not involve re-enactment in Collingwood's sense, but seems to be an example of history.[7] We might think that history is a matter of interpretation in the same way that causation is a matter of intervention. Not all causal relationships involve an intervention, but we can understand causal relationships *because* we understand what it is to intervene. Similarly, not all history is the interpretation of the actions of others (including spoken and written actions), but we can understand how technological developments (for example) might lead to social changes, because we understand what it is to interpret the meaningfulness of actions.

Narratives are useful to history because they allow that the events of history are contingent one-offs. They allow that the events of history might only make sense in retrospect. Various historical events change from being unimaginable to inevitable in a short period of time, and narratives allow us to see both what it was like not to know where the plot was headed (since we can see from the protagonists' point of view) and to see how each step in a story led inexorably to its conclusion.

METANARRATIVE AND POSTMODERNISM

Historical narratives tell stories about the past. Some of them are quite local stories, and some of them are more general. We can, as in the previous two sentences, talk about what we are doing when we talk about the past. That is, we can have narratives about narratives, or 'metanarratives' as they are sometimes called.

Some narratives make grand claims about historical narratives generally. The Whig interpretation of history was a view by some

18th and 19th century British Historians that the History of England was one of the rise of scientific progress, constitutional government, personal freedom.

If the history of England isn't sweeping enough, G.W.F. Hegel thought that *all* history was a process of rationally working out tensions to arrive at some definite end point: The Absolute. Hegel was far from the only person to do this, but represented the most thoroughly worked out version of the view that history is *going somewhere*. Not only is history going somewhere, but it is making moral progress, in which the world gets better until perfecting itself.

Hegel was very influential in promoting this idea of moral progress, but also influenced other people who defended their own metanarratives of moral progress. Karl Marx's 'dialectical materialism' owes a strong debt to Hegel. The end point of history in global communism is a specific version of Hegel's dialectic, based on the working through tensions in the economic means of production to their inevitable conclusion. Francis Fukuyama, by contrast, takes Western Liberal Democracy to be the 'end of history'. Societies, once they work out the inherent contradictions in their way of operating, will naturally end at an equilibrium. That equilibrium is different for Hegel, Marx, and Fukuyama, but in each case, defenders claim, it is the inevitable conclusion of a grand meta-narrative that individual narrative histories are smaller contributions to.

Two things that made many historians sceptical of grand-meta-narratives of moral progress – often derided as '*whig history*' – are World War One and World War Two. It was simply very difficult to fit the industrial slaughter of the Battle of the Somme and the systematic extermination of millions of people using industrial efficiency of the Holocaust into a metanarrative of continuing moral progress. Nonetheless, Fukuyama's article 'The End of History' was published in 1989. He was aware of concerns about Hegelian views of history.

Metanarratives need not take this heroic form, but could be the tragic decline of civilisation as a result of hubris, or the satiric attempt to dream that human nature can be overcome, or many others besides. An alternative is to reject metanarratives altogether. *Postmodernism* is a philosophical movement that rejects the idea that there is coherent sense to be made out of things taken as a whole. We're not going to find a single True (with a capital 'T') account of the world, that gives an objective and unbiased view. Jean-François Lyotard, one of the advocates of postmodernism, describes it as follows: 'Simplifying to the extreme, I define *postmodern* as incredulity towards metanarratives' (1979/2001:xxiv).

There is good reason to be suspicious of confidence that a particular theorist, political party or religious sect has found *the* correct meta-narrative. The confidence in which someone claims to know how history is going to go in advance seems to underestimate the significance of the asymmetry of records discussed in chapter 6. Our ability to predict is nowhere near as good as our ability to investigate what actually happened. And if we are sufficiently confident in advance of where history is heading, we may be inattentive to evidence that contradicts this prediction. Or worse, perhaps, we may make excuses for our heroes rather than see them as much more morally ambiguous figures.

During the 1956 Hungarian Revolution, the Soviet Union sent tanks into Hungary to crush the uprising. Such was the confidence in Soviet leader Joseph Stalin as the embodiment of the inevitable triumph of global communism, many communists defended the use of tanks to put down the revolution as a necessary and proportionate use of force. Those communists who felt that Stalin's sending in the tanks was indefensible started calling their opponents 'tankies'. The term persists as a description of those who are prepared to defend brutal repression of resistance to their utopian political vision. Although the ideologies and regimes change, the capacity of people to reinterpret the evidence to fit their beliefs is still widely observable.

One response to the postmodern incredulity at metanarratives is to treat them as poses one adopts temporarily, or as lenses through which one chooses, for certain purposes, to look. That is, the postmodernist may find themselves unable to take seriously any *commitment* to a worldview. The warnings of history show that excessive confidence in a metanarrative is to be avoided, but it doesn't so clearly speak against a more tentative use of metanarratives as working hypotheses.

The different ways of approaching history are not all equally valuable. And the historian, like any skilled inquirer, needs to have some sense of what they are aiming to do, and what it is to do that well. I worry that talk of 'lenses' or 'stances' often disguises what

Susan Haack (1998) calls 'sham-inquiry'. Sham-inquiry is where there is the appearance of an attempt to find something out, but with the conclusion set in advance. If metanarratives are merely taken up for rhetorical effect, without some question about whether they are suitable tools for the present investigation, the investigation isn't a genuine inquiry, Haack argues.

Narratives can explain why the passage of time from the point of view of explaining history looks very different from explaining the passage of time in physics. History is doubly hermeneutic and involves narratives that allow us to make sense of actions and events as being caught between a past and future that is open to interpretation and reinterpretation in light of different foregrounding of things as significant. These might be past things, potential future things, or even collectively imagined things. Given that history is doubly hermeneutic, we might be *accurately* or *inaccurately* attempting to interpret people who themselves might be accurate or inaccurate. We shall turn now to consider what the constraint that history aims to be accurate amounts to.

REALISM AND ANTI-REALISM ABOUT HISTORY

If at the start of a film it says 'inspired by a true story' that usually means that most of what you will see and hear will be fiction. There will be some relation to actual events – 'inspiration' – but this is not nearly the same as saying that the story depicted is true. What is it for a story to be true, though?

'True' gets used in a number of different senses. We might have a story composed entirely of true sentences that we want to describe as false, because it omits so much of significance as to be actively misleading. We can equally see an entirely fictional story performed by a skilled actor and say that they brought real truth and sincerity to the role, even though they didn't believe that they were Prince of Denmark, or whatever. Occasionally, when people are describing their personal experience, they are encouraged to 'speak their truth', as if truth were something that we each had our own private supply of.

Aristotle ('Metaphysics' *IV.7*, 1011b25) characterises truth in the following way: 'to say of what is that it is not, or of what is not that it is, is false, while to say of what is that it is, and of what is not that it is not, is true'. A straightforward way to ask the question of whether some historical narrative is true is to ask if it meets Aristotle's criteria. Does it say of what is that it is, and what is not that it is not?

Obviously, the problem here is that historical narratives are always going to be partial. They always omit somethings and foreground some things against the background of other things. A commitment to truth is an admission that not just any narrative will do; historical narratives are constrained by the past. In criticising Shakespeare's *Julius Caesar*, it seems open to you to complain 'but that's not how things happened' in a way that would just be missing the point for *The Tempest*. We can't compare Shakespeare's Prospero to the real one, in the way we can compare the character Julius Caesar to the historically recorded one.

This constraint can be quite easily met. We can create a 'true history' very easily by making a narrative so general that it is almost empty:

> In the past, a series of events occurred, some of which led to the current situation.

We might prefer a narrative that occasionally says false things but goes into considerably more detail, for example. We also might prefer that a few complications are removed to aid understanding. But *amongst* the things that a historian does, when they are being a historian, is to try to get the past right. If they are not guided by that as an aim, they are simply not doing history, but writing historical fiction, or allegories or something.

We may also think of truth as *correspondence to the facts*. In a weak sense, this might just be a redescription of Aristotle's criteria, but it's helpful to think about how 'correspondence' and 'facts' might create some problems. Then we'll get on to the really dangerous word: 'the'.

Imagine someone doing a comparison between two sets of lists: a list of narrative sentences from a historian, and a list of facts about the past. They might think that a historical narrative is true when each sentence of the narrative corresponds to a sentence on the list of facts. The problem here is thinking that 'the past' in any way resembles a list of facts.

Is the world made of facts, rather than things? Does the world come structured with narratives waiting to be uttered? Some philosophers have thought so.[8] But you might think that the world does not come pre-packaged in the form of a totality of facts, but rather as something that we have invented methods to characterise in various ways for various purposes. The language of physics may be one such language, but it is not more privileged than the poet's language, just more highly prescriptive. We might compliment a good poem for getting the world right in some way, even if it does so solely through a series of metaphors that are literally false.

Let's accept that history must aim to get the past right (even if it needn't always succeed to count as history). One way to get the world right is to create some facts, and then, because we have just created them, we can describe that bit of the world we have just created. Some historians think that what they do when they do history is create some historical facts in the course of doing history. Let's call this view *constructivism*.

Constructivism, in an extreme form, is obviously dangerously wrong. If the Party Historians decide that the Official Version of History is to be taught in all schools and promulgated in all newspapers, that doesn't seem like what happened is now whatever the Official Version of History says happened. At an extreme, constructivism ignores the central need of history to be constrained by the past. Not just any narrative can be constructed, and the test is not what the Party Historians can get away with, or what the extant evidence shows. If it were, then a sufficiently totalitarian Party could meet that test. The test is whether the Official Version of History does a good job of describing what happened.

But constructivism needn't be so extreme. Take the English revolution of 1688, for example. It was a series of events that occurred, some of which led to our current situation. That it *counts* as a revolution may be something that historians get to decide, by creating a system of classification that puts different sequences of events together as being of the same kind.

History, as we've said, is doubly hermeneutic. That means that not only does it involve human attempts to make sense of their lives, but human attempts to make sense of human attempts to make sense of their lives. In the course of this sense-making we can create social entities: nations, empires, intellectual movements, political parties, governments, trades unions, rebellions, revolutions, economic systems, corporations, businesses, genders, races, disabilities, sexualities and academic disciplines. As creators of these things, we do a lot of work to make them the things that they are, rather than merely discovering them as features of the world.

The constructivist is right to point out that these things are human artefacts and that the historian is complicit in making them what they are. What a social entity *is* depends on how it narratively understands itself, because it uses those narratives to work out how to continue into the future. Although they are created by conventions, practices and narratives, social entities become part of reality as much as anything else. Social constructions are never the creation of an individual who decides that they are changing the meaning of a bunch of words, but a collective agreement to understand a form of words in a particular way. Even once we accept that race or gender are socially contingent categories, that could change if society redefined them (as opposed to phenotype and sex which are biological classifications, for example), one person cannot decide that they are redefining their role in that system without the cooperation of other users of that system.

For at least some bits of the world, then, the constructivist must be right that they are social artefacts. But we should avoid going from that acceptance to thinking that the constraint of getting things right is a constraint only to tell consistent stories about the worlds we create. Those social worlds are based in a reality we share and built out of that reality.

Realism is the view that historians *discover* rather than create historical facts. That is, this is the view (which I have been presupposing throughout) that there *is* a constraint on the narratives historians tell, such that the narratives are true *because* of how the world is, and not that the world is how it is *because* the historians describe it that way. The realist might accept in particular domains that we're dealing with human artefacts, but not that the subject matter of physics is human artefacts, even if the equipment physicists use is, and the practice of studying physics is.

At its extreme, realism also runs into trouble, however. The temptation to believe that the historian can find a version of history that is final, because it, unlike others, *gets things right* comes from a mistaken belief that the constraint on narratives that they 'get things right' narrows the options down to a single true narrative. But as we observed above, choices about what to include and what to omit, what to foreground, where to begin, and where to end are routine. If you discuss the causes of the American Civil War without mentioning the dispute about whether Kansas would permit slave-ownership, it seems you've missed something really important. If we accept that there are multiple choices allowed by the constraint that the historian must get the past right, then there will be many options on which of those choices to make.

What's more, a realist who takes the difficulty of history seriously will be aware that they are likely to fail to get things right because of various biases that, because they are widely shared by their society, they are unable to see. Taking the need to get things right seriously involves always being open to criticism from a perspective you have not yet considered. It's not just that history can be re-told many ways, but we can learn something from the various retellings to do *better* next time.

QUESTIONS FOR DISCUSSION

1. In what sense, if any, can you change the past after it's happened?
2. Are there literary forms that the historian cannot make use of?
3. What constraint does 'getting the past right' place on a historian?
4. What biases are you likely to bring to the historical narratives you tell?
5. How does the scale at which historians describe things affect what they include in their histories?

NOTES

1 Some languages make the useful distinction between past historical events and the description of those events, e.g. '*Geschichte*' and '*Historie*' in German.
2 Walter Gallie (1964), Roland Barthes (1981/1967), Louis Mink (1970), for example. But notice how I'm condensing down the complex movement to revive narrative in history to a key figure foregrounded against a background of others. This is a narrative decision that will inevitably reveal something about my concerns as an author as much as reveal anything about the philosophical landscape.

3 Bias, here, in the pejorative sense that it fails to demonstrate the appropriate objectivity.

4 That I have foregrounded this cultural reference, against *all* the others I could have chosen, is clearly a significant choice. But it stands out for being a low-brow, and dated, cultural reference for an academic textbook. The choice to include the Annals of St Gall is no less significant, but signifies something else.

   Aristotle's 'The Parts of Animals' (645a17–23) has an anecdote about some travellers who visit Heraclitus, who was a famous philosopher in Ancient Greece. The visitors find Heraclitus warming himself by the stove in the kitchen, and hesitate to go in. Heraclitus replies 'Come inside. There are gods here too'. Aristotle takes the lesson to be to find philosophical interest in humble things, such as the biology of small animals. To this I add, there is philosophical interest even in comedy sequels of the 1990s.

5 The whodunnit for instance.

6 Collingwood (1946/1994)

7 He would be interested in how people understood the printing-press. There's a story about why and in what circumstances people came to realise the potential of the printing press. But that isn't the same as pointing out that the printing press increased the bandwidth of information that could be transmitted by groups opposed to the governing regime.

8 Cf. Wittgenstein (1922/1965: §1.1)

FURTHER READING

White (1980) outlines the different emplotments that we might place on history.

Danto (1985) defends history as a narrative enterprise.

Day (2008) gives an introductory overview of a range of issues in the philosophy of history.

LIVING IN THE PRESENT

We have considered a range of issues about the flow of time, and the direction of time. In the previous chapter we considered the challenges for historians of explaining the events in time. This chapter is focused on the challenges for us as individuals. We are creatures of time, and we live our lives in it. Eventually, we end our lives in time. We ask a number of philosophical questions in the course of our lives:

- When can we say a life is well lived?
- What's the harm in ceasing to be?
- Can I promise to feel this way in the future?
- What might have been, if I had done otherwise?

Philosophy of time ought to have something to say about these issues. Indeed, armed with the topics from previous chapters, we'll consider what it might say about these questions, and finish by considering the relationship between some of these questions and the more theoretical questions of earlier in the book.

SOLON'S PROBLEM

When can we say that someone's life is going well? Solon, an ancient Athenian statesman, claimed that you should call no-one happy until they are dead, on the basis that a sudden change of fortune could still affect them. Aristotle pushed the point further: death was far too soon to know whether a life had gone well. After all, changes of fortune could still happen after death.[1]

DOI: 10.4324/9781003189459-11

Aristotle finds it puzzling that what's happened after someone's death should affect how well their life has gone, but equally finds it implausible that various things they have achieved in their life (such as bringing up children and marrying them well) could be suddenly undone shortly after their death without it affecting our assessment of their life. This problem, of how and when we assess how a life is going, is one of the main topics of this chapter. Before we get into this problem, we need to consider another. Is death bad for us?

IS DEATH BAD FOR US?

It's important to clarify this question. Firstly, it's asking whether death is bad for the person who dies. It is quite clearly bad for loved ones who grieve the death. Secondly, it's important to distinguish the matter of not being alive any more from the process of dying. Dying can be traumatic and painful in its own right, or it can be quick, painless, and unexpected. There are important questions about what it is for someone to have a good death (i.e. for the process leading up to death to be the best process it can be). Here we are concerned with whether it is bad for the person who dies to not be around anymore. Finally, we are assuming that death is the permanent end of life. In this sense of death, it makes no sense for someone to be dead for two minutes before being revived.

Epicurus, the Ancient Greek founder of the Epicurean school of philosophy, advised that there was no harm in death:

> Accustom yourself to believe that death is nothing to us. For all good and evil lie in sensation, whereas death is the absence of sensation… Therefore that most frightful of evils, is nothing to us, seeing that when we exist death is not present, and when death is present, we do not exist.[2]

Epicurus' account is refreshingly straightforward. And his reason has the direct consequence that we can't be harmed *after* our death for the same reason we can't be harmed by our death, viz. we will not be there. As the quote makes clear, the reasoning relies on an assumption that the only things that affect whether life goes well or ill is sensation, by which he means pleasure and pain. This view, that the only things that matter are pleasure and pain is called '**hedonism**'.

The term is popularly associated with risk-taking pleasure seekers. Epicurus in fact argued for finding pleasure in simple natural things so that you could attain pleasure easily and it wouldn't cause pain later by becoming addictive, or creating desires that were impossible to satisfy. As I am using 'hedonism', it is the ethical claim about what matters, rather than the psychological claim that pleasure and pain is all that motivates people.

The problem with hedonism is that it looks to be false: pleasure and pain aren't the only things that make life go well or ill. Or at least, very few people are prepared to accept that those are the only two things that allow life to go well or ill. Here's a quick test of whether you're a hedonist. Would it be bad if all the people you thought were your friends were laughing at you behind your back, even if you never found out? The hedonist has to say that it is the finding out that is bad, but what doesn't cause you pain can't be bad for you.

If you accept that it is bad to be mistaken in who your friends are, it's not a big step to accept that your life can go badly after your death. Those same friends could like you while you are alive and then come to dislike you after your death. You will definitely not find out about it (being dead), but it will be bad to lose those friends nonetheless.

Hedonism is useful if you like decision theory, as discussed in chapter 8. If the values that go into the decision problems are amounts of pleasure and pain, it seems more plausible that it is possible to maximise pleasure or minimise pain than to know how to trade off a much richer range of values. Trading pleasure and pain off between people or across times is still problematic, but hedonism is nonetheless commonly associated with ethical theories that treat ethical decision making as a calculation of various quantities of pleasure and pain.

If we don't accept hedonism, what can explain the badness of death? A common answer is provided by **deprivation** accounts. Death is bad because it deprives someone of something that they would otherwise have had. What it deprives them of is a future in which they could have had more good things, contributed more to society, and achieved more things that matter. On this sort of view the badness of death depends on what would have happened had they not died.

If it is possible to be harmed by one's own death, let's think about the case where we are harmed by something after we die. John O'Neill (1993) has an argument that it *is* possible to harmed after death. He uses an example of William Rowan Hamilton:

> William Rowan Hamilton did work on optics that has come to be very important in quantum theory. He spent the last 20 years of his life working on 'quaternions' which he thought would be his major achievement. Quaternions were not the achievement Hamilton thought they would be. They played a role in the development of vector analysis, but several features Hamilton thought were particularly important were put to one side. Recently, however, a Chinese physicist, Li He, published a paper using quaternions in a way that helps solve some of the paradoxes in quantum mechanics. It looks like the last 20 years of Hamilton's life were not wasted after all!

O'Neill then goes on to point out that the stuff about the recent discovery is total fiction. Li He is not real and quaternions weren't used to solve the paradoxes of quantum mechanics. But the discovery of some important application for the work seems to change how Hamilton's life went. Not just by changing how useful that work was, but by vindicating his own assessment of the value of that work which was viewed as being a waste of time by his contemporaries. Some future development changes the whole narrative of Hamilton's life.

It is pleasingly ironic that since O'Neill's article in 1993, quaternions really have come to be widely recognised as very useful. Specifically in computer graphics processing, and the control of spacecraft. These are applications that rely on computational systems that Hamilton was incapable of imagining, but he deserves credit for having developed the mathematical tools to achieve those things. His achievement in developing that mathematical theory *has* changed since his death!

One of the key things to emphasise about this example is it is not meant to show that Hamilton's reputation can change, but that Hamilton's *achievement* can change. The idea is that how well our lives go is a matter, in part, of what we achieve during them. And doing foundational work that never gets built upon is a different achievement to doing foundational work that allows for great things.

THE OZYMANDIAS PROBLEM

Perhaps the solution is to abstract ourselves from particular moments in time, and take a longer view of time. But that has its own problems. Given a long enough duration, it is easy to think that anything we might achieve might not really matter. The hedonist has the advantage that what matters is what matters to us right now. If you think that what matters is an objective matter, you may have to consider the possibility that nothing any of us achieves matters.

Christopher Bennett (2010) illustrates this with the example of Percy Shelley's poem *Ozymandias*.[3] In the poem, a traveller comes across a ruined statue in the desert bearing the inscription:

> My name is Ozymandias, King of Kings;
> Look on my Works, ye Mighty, and despair!

This is clearly the statue of a great emperor (Ancient Egyptian emperor Ramesses II, in fact). But his works have all turned to dust except fragments of a statue. Even the mightiest of us will not have achievements that last forever. Given how brief, on a cosmic timescale, human life has existed so far, getting the measure of achievements at that scale is hard to do. As Thomas Nagel (1986:210) puts it: 'to see myself objectively as a small, contingent, and exceedingly temporary organic bubble in the universal soup produces an attitude approaching indifference.'

The challenge of assessing when our lives are going well is one which has no fixed timescale. In the early 1970s Zhou Enlai, a Chinese statesman, was reported to respond to American Stateman Henry Kissinger's question about whether the French Revolution was a good thing by remarking that it was 'too early to say'.[4] This open-endedness is important, because it makes the question of how well our lives go an objective one, and not a question of our own opinion. Nagel (1979:5) discusses the case of 'the man who wastes his life in the cheerful pursuit of a method of communicating with asparagus plants' as an example of someone who thinks they are leading a good life, but are objectively not. The Hamilton example is meant to show a commitment to thinking that some activities are objectively more valuable than others. While it is often wise not to vocally judge how others spend their time, in the decisions we make about our own lives, and in the advice we give our friends, we tend to take seriously the idea that some ways of spending one's time are better than others.

The moral assessment of our lives has an open-endedness, though of course not *all* events in our lives will be ambiguous as to whether they are good or not. If I spend time with a friend, and we both enjoy ourselves, it seems as though that activity has value regardless of its consequences. Even if our lives depend on luck, even after our death, much of what makes a life go well is something in our own hands. Spending time doing things we enjoy, are good at, and benefit others is a reasonably safe bet when it comes to living well.

RETROSPECTION, NOSTALGIA AND MELANCHOLY

Even if our life is going well, we can find that certain feelings arise. We can find our thoughts drawn with nostalgia to times when we were younger, or with melancholy towards a future where things won't be the same again.

Attar of Nishapur, a Sufi poet from the turn of the 12th/13th centuries, has a fable in which a powerful king is in a melancholy mood and asks for his sages to make him a magic ring with a curious property: it must make a sad man happy and a happy man sad. After considerable deliberation, the sages create a simple gold ring with an inscription. The inscription reads 'This too shall pass'.

If life is going well, simply the knowledge that it is temporary can induce a state of melancholy. If things are going badly, the knowledge that it is temporary can induce hope. What's striking about this is that one's emotional state can appear to become disconnected from how well one's life is going. People are content to endure great hardships if they think that there will be a later reward for it. And people can feel miserable despite having achieved their goals, because they think that the best is behind them. Things can get more complicated than this, as people can feel sad about things that didn't happen but could have, and nostalgic towards things that never were.

Nostalgia, in particular, is interesting because it typically involves a longing for a past that never happened. It is a longing for the good old days that tends to rely on a very selective memory of what the old days were like, and what made them good.[5] In the case of naïve optimism about the future, it is an implausible view of what things are going to be like, but given how hard the future is to predict, the naïve optimist is only guilty of making implausible inferences from how things are now. In the case of nostalgia, we have records of what things were like that can directly contradict some of the more idealised versions of history that people are emotionally attached to. As we saw in the previous chapter, working out how to constrain our historical narratives is difficult. But one of the reasons we need to is because the emotional pull of nostalgia can make learning from our mistakes difficult. To learn from them, we need to acknowledge that there is something from which to learn.

Keiran Setiya (2016:2) looks at another puzzle of feeling emotions directed towards the past:

> Alive in my reflection are the lives I have not led. When I think about them, when I imagine them vividly, I can be gripped by something like regret: a sense of loss. I do not believe I would have a lived a better life in poetry or medicine; most likely, worse. And yet I feel dissatisfied with how things are. I look back with envy at my younger self, options open, choices not yet made. He could be anything. But I am committed: course set, path fixed, doors closed.

The thought here is that we can feel a sense of loss by no longer having the choices we had when we were younger, *even if we think we made the right choices*. Setiya suggests that we feel having the options is good, regardless of what the options are. This picks up one of the themes of chapter 7; that we think that the future is in some sense open whereas the past is not. Now of course Setiya still thinks it matters what the options are; we prefer to have good options to bad options, after all. But there's no question it's possible to feel stuck or caged if you don't have options to choose amongst, even if the options left are all good ones.

There's a parallel here with existential dread. Luca Banfi (2021) argues that existential dread requires the passage of time. This seems to be because having options can be both pleasant and dreadful. On the one hand, it is very exciting to have one's future in one's hands. But this excitement can very easily bubble over into fear. If one doesn't know whether or not things will turn out alright, the capacity for being the one who totally mucks everything up is quite scary.

As Setiya points out, it's true just after one has made a big decision that it's all still to come. But it's the time immediately before the decision that is most exciting/scary. There's something about finding oneself in the decisive moment that feels very different to the moments before or after the decision. This suggests that there is some change going on besides what time it is. For myself, I think it is a change from potentiality to actuality, as outlined in chapters 6 and 7, but it might be that it is merely a change in our information. *Feeling* like the situation has changed might be all there is to it.

NARRATIVES OF OUR LIVES

We saw in the previous chapter, narratives have the interesting property that the narrative as a whole can change by adding on an extra chapter. Just as histories of others and of states and nations can be emplotted, we can narrate our own lives to ourselves. And when we do so, order effects seem to matter. A rags to riches story seems better than a riches to rags story, even if the average quality of life across the life is the same.

The narratives we tell ourselves during our lives are significant. The goals we set ourselves will depend on the assessments of what we are capable of. Someone who tells themselves that they aren't good enough may strive for more constantly; they may go on to achieve impressive feats. But it will never be enough. Someone who thinks of themselves as one of the world's born losers is likely to be right; it's a narrative others find off-putting.

As with history, there is some constraint to our narratives. Sometimes the world will contradict the story that you tell yourself in ways you cannot ignore. But often there are feedback effects where doing things confidently makes them more likely to succeed, and assuming a stranger is a friend you haven't met yet makes it much easier to make friends. Given that how your life goes isn't settled yet, the question of how to narrate it to yourself is difficult to answer. How you narrate your life to yourself is one of the biggest things that you can do to affect how it goes! Proponents of positive psychology recommend a practice of continually finding a positive way to narrate things. Every challenge is an opportunity, every failure is a learning opportunity, and every day you are alive is a reason to be grateful. Seen up close, those who practice this can be very impressive, and often get a lot done. There's a risk, however, that a focus on the positive can lead to a fear of the negative. The stories that we tell ourselves are often quite fragile, and investing heavily in those stories can make us quite vulnerable.

In chapter 4, we encountered a special concern for the future as a reason to believe that there is McTchange. Our feelings of retrospective sadness, melancholy and existential dread seem to be related to that concern for *our* future, and what is or isn't *up to us*. We can see here how the questions in this chapter about how we live are relevant to metaphysical questions about the nature of time.[6] One such question concerns the role of narratives and selves.

There's a view that what a person *is* is something constituted by a certain sort of narration. We 'self-constitute' – literally create ourselves – by narrating our lives to ourselves. It is our having a narrative that makes sense of our past as leading into our future that allows for the 'diachronic unity of agency' that allows us to be moral agents. What 'diachronic unity of agency' means, is that we are able to act as a single agent over time. So, the stories we tell ourselves about who we are and what we are doing over time, on this view, are what make us the kind of things that can carry out actions, and be praised, blamed, compensated or sanctioned for the actions we carry out.

We might question whether we need just a single unfolding narrative for our lives, however. There's an argument, originating with Aristotle, articulated by Alasdair MacIntyre (2006:192–3) that argues that we need to have a unitary self to be a morally good person:

> To have integrity is to refuse to be, to have educated oneself so that one is no longer able to be, one kind of person in one social context, while quite another in other contexts. It is to have set inflexible limits to one's adaptability to the roles that one may be called upon to play. Constancy, like integrity, sets limits to flexibility of character. Where integrity requires of those who possess it, that they exhibit the same moral character in different social contexts, constancy requires that

those who possess it pursue the same goods through extended periods of time, not allowing the requirements of changing social context to distract them from their commitments.

MacIntyre's view doesn't strictly require one narrative, but is the
view that there needs to be a unity of character to possess integrity.
Constancy seems related to consistency, as discussed in chapter 8. If
we think people's characters are created by them through their own
narratives, those narratives would need a unity to them as well.

Not everyone is convinced. We often have narratives that are
fragmentary; indeed these are characteristic of a certain kind of modern literary fiction. Just as modern fiction contains fragmentary narratives, modern people might narrative fragmentary selves. Genevieve
Lloyd (1993) argues that the demands on modern city-dwelling people are too great to expect us to have unified narratives in this way.
Keiran Setiya (2022:100) puts his objection like this:

> there is a downside to unified, linear narrative: it is by squeezing your
> life into a single tube that you set yourself up for definitive failure…
> When you define your life by way of a single enterprise, a narrative
> arc, its outcome will come to define *you*.

Neither Lloyd nor Setiya object to the idea that we use narrative
forms to make sense of our lives, but the aim of *unity*, even if it
allows for virtues of constancy and integrity, has a tendency to force
us into a story that we can't help but overflow. Similarly, to have a
sense of one's present as held hostage by an uncertain future in
which *the* narrative of one's life gets settled is likely to make one
anxious. Setiya recommends a focus on living in the present, not by
ignoring the future, but by concentrating on doing activities that
are valuable in themselves rather than because of the achievements
that they may or may not come to represent. On his view we should
leave the grand narratives to the historians and get on with living.

OATHS

The assessment of how well our life is going is open-ended, but we
don't often wait and see what we will do. We often plan, and coordinate plans with others. In fact, one thing we do is make promise

to others so that they rely on us in the future, and solicit promises from others so that we may rely on them. But given how changeable our circumstances are, and we ourselves are, isn't there something problematic about promising for a future that we can't predict?

PROMISES AND OATHS

We often make promises. Some promises are pretty minor ones. I promise to run some errand or other. It might be inconvenient if I forget, get waylaid, or it turns out the promise is unfulfillable. For most people the inconvenience is pretty minor, and an apology or an excuse will be the end of the matter. In these cases, making a promise is more-or-less a way of being slightly more emphatic in expressing an intention to do something. In other cases, we think that promises are to be taken rather seriously. The failure to keep one's promises might have serious consequences, and might also seriously damage the trust that exists between the promise-maker and the person the promise was made to.

Often, if you make a promise, you can be released from it by someone else. Also, some promises stop applying if the circumstances change sufficiently (such that you could keep the promise, but it would be unreasonable to expect it to be kept). If you owe someone money, they might forgive the debt. If they forgive the debt, you don't still have to pay them the money. If you promise to bake someone a cake, and then your house burns down, you technically could find another kitchen in which to bake the cake, but we might think it unreasonable for you to be bound by that promise given that it was made when you expected easy access to a kitchen. In such cases we might describe you as 'excused' from keeping the promise; you didn't have to keep the promise because you had an excuse.

There are various conditions that making a promise involves. Here is a list based on one from J.L. Austin (1962):[7]

A1 There has to be an agreed method of promising.
A2 The person and the circumstances have to be right for promising.
B1 The person must do something which constitutes the act of promising.

B2   They must complete the act of promising.
Γ. **1**   They need to be sincere.
Γ. **2**   They need to keep the promise.

Working through that list, promising is not something you can do by accident; what *counts* as making a promise has to be agreed when the promise is made. That agreement will involve various conditions. For one thing, the promise-maker has to have the authority to make the promise. I can't promise things on behalf of someone whom I am not authorised to represent. If I (attempt to) promise something on behalf of the Canadian people, it simply won't count as a promise because I'm not in a position to collectively bind Canadians. Circumstances might matter too. A promise made in a court of law is legally binding in a way the same form of words in different circumstances (for instance by an actor in a play) doesn't count as a promise at all. A1 and A2 have to do with whether something *counts* as a promise, then.

B1 and B2 have to do with whether the promise was carried out correctly. So, whatever the procedures are, the person making the promise must do something that follows such a procedure, and they have to correctly follow the procedure to the end. If they don't do this, we might say that they attempted to make a promise but didn't succeed, either due to a flaw in the procedure followed, or a hitch in carrying it out.

Γ. 1 and Γ. 2 are slightly different. The other conditions are about what is needed for a promise to be successfully made, and these are about whether a promise is appropriately made. An insincere promise still counts as a promise, but it is an abuse of the institution of promise-keeping to follow the procedure intending not to keep the promise. Similarly, even if you sincerely make a promise, you also have to keep it. It is an abuse of promise keeping as an institution to really intend to keep a promise and then forget or change your mind later. As Katherine Hawley (2020) pointed out, the over-enthusiastic person who takes on more commitments than they can honour is untrustworthy as much as the insincere person.

I want to think about the more morally serious promises, and those more morally serious promises where you can't be released from them by someone else, and you will be held to them regardless of changes in circumstances. I will call this special category of promises '**oaths**'. In the traditional terminology of oaths, you 'take' an oath by 'swearing' it, and if you 'break' the oath, you are in the undesirable position of being 'forsworn'. This being a special category of promise, it might be that you should never swear an oath, and instead stick to the kind of promises that you can be excused from or released from.

We've discussed the ways in which people change through transformative experiences already in chapters 8 and 9. In chapter 8 we were concerned with decision making, and in chapter 9 with interpreting history. Now we are concerned with a different but related issue: *voluntarily permanently binding* ourselves in the future. If making oaths has to be voluntary (oaths made under duress violate condition A1), and oaths are by definition permanently binding (since unlike other promises, we can't be released from them, or excused due to change in circumstances), does it make sense to sincerely swear oaths knowing that we and the world around us will change over time?

There's obviously something useful about swearing unbreakable oaths. If there is something very important that you don't want to change, creating a binding promise that someone will stop it changing is very useful. Coronation oaths, for example, involve getting a commitment from the monarch being crowned to rule in a certain way. Let's set aside the complexities of modern constitutional monarchies for a moment and think about the case where you hand over absolute sovereign power to an individual for life. Their taking an oath publicly in a special ceremony to use that power in a certain way commits them. Because they are being given sovereign power, there is no-one who can relieve them of their promise later; they have absolute executive power.

Given this absolute power they might have the authority to relieve themselves of their own promises later. But an oath is precisely meant to be a kind of promise that one can't be relieved of later. Oaths are useful, then, to have a check on absolute power. In practice, it might not stop them. But they invite others' moral contempt if they forswear themselves. Rulers do best when they aren't held in contempt by those they govern.

Deathbed promises look a lot like oaths. The person who dies immediately after extracting a promise might be the only person capable of lifting the promise. If they get you to promise to look after their children, you're morally on the hook for the children. If you are unwise enough to promise that you will look after the children *no matter what*, that's going to be an oath, as I have been using the term. While we can see that someone on their deathbed concerned for their children might wish to get you to commit in this way, is it ever sensible for you to commit yourself?

One consideration that might be helpful is thinking about what sort of thing is getting promised. Promises to behave in a certain way might be different from promises to believe certain things and promises to feel a certain way. There's a view that beliefs and emotions are not under one's control, only behaviour is. The driving thought here is that beliefs are not things we choose. We believe according to the evidence as it appears to us. If we have compelling evidence that something is false, we can't choose to think it true, even if it would be helpful if we did. Similarly, if we feel a certain way about something, or someone, changing those feelings, or continuing to feel them, isn't just something we can choose to do. Since we can only promise to do those things that are up to us, we can't promise to believe something come what may, or to feel something come what may.

If you are persuaded by that reasoning, then that rules out a swathe of oaths from being ones you can swear. You can't swear to believe in any religious doctrine, to love someone for the rest of your life, to disbelieve any accusation or to never feel this way again. The best you can do is to act as though you believe or feel a certain way.

You may resist the reasoning I have just presented. Although feeling and believing things is not something that you can just decide to do, you are not powerless. If you wish to continue to believe something, it's best to avoid exposure to sources of evidence you know will make you doubt. If you wish not to feel things, avoid going into situations you know are likely to provoke such feelings. Although you can't directly control your feelings, you have considerable control over the sorts of influences that do. You can direct your attention to features that make the belief seem plausible or the emotion seem appropriate.

Troy Jollimore, writing about love, points out that this situation is in fact more complicated than I have so far presented it. Usually, we are in a situation where there are a plurality of reasons to feel various ways. It's not that the situations we are presented with permit of only one compelling response. Someone can see that two people are both attractive, but only pay attention to one of them. What's more we can make commitments to one another in terms of ways that we will pay attention to the world. If there's some kind of transformative experience that changes what you value in really profound ways, that will naturally affect what you believe and how you feel. Perhaps swearing unbreakable oaths to love someone is always unwise, but one can make commitments. These commitments, to Jollimore, are commitments to *seeing* the beloved in a certain way, as (at least potentially) a source of certain kinds of value. Although one may cease, in the short or long-term, to find a source of value there, the commitment (indeed the habit) of looking for it is very important. As he warns us:

> But love is unlikely to survive if one too frequently engages in serious questionings of this sort. Anyone who has been engaged in a long-term love relationship will know that serious reconsiderations of one's commitment, particularly if they are brought out into the open and shared with one's partner, tend to be disturbing if not traumatic.[8]

With belief too, it may be that we can't bind ourself to finding the evidence compelling, but we may have a commitment not to re-open investigation into the evidence. Believing things, and feelings things may not be an infinite sequence of decisions about what to think or feel, but neither are they an infinite sequence of exposures to a tribunal of experience. We can often treat questions as closed, and we can often avoid potentially transformative experiences that we fear may re-open them.[9]

ODYSSEUS PROTOCOLS

We have seen it can be useful for others to bind us. There are some situations in which it is clear why we should wish to be bound. In Homer's *Odyssey*, there are some creatures called 'sirens' that sing beautifully, luring passing sailors to their death onto the rocks. The title character of the *Odyssey*, Odysseus, has been warned he will be sailing past the sirens, so has his crew put in some earplugs made of wax, so they can't hear the sirens. But because he wants to hear the song himself, he has himself bound (with ropes) to the mast of his ship. He gives his sailors instructions not to release him until they have passed the sirens, *no matter how much he begs them*. In this case, Odysseus is getting the sailors to swear an oath not to release him. The sailors cannot be released from their promise by Odysseus, and the circumstances for freeing him are fully explicit. But Odysseus is physically bound to experience the siren's song, and cannot withdraw his consent to the plan. He is bound to follow the course of action he set out on, regardless of what he feels later.

'Odysseus protocols' are procedures where someone binds themself for a specified future period, so that they cannot change their decision for the duration of that period, no matter what they say. These can come in various forms, but usually involve an instruction that countermanding future instructions be ignored, just as in the case of Odysseus and the sirens. These can be very useful if someone is entering a situation of extreme temptation, or is attempting to overcome an addiction. They give permission to one's friends (or those acting on one's behalf) to ignore or override your wishes, which normally they would be required to respect. They can be very sensible for situations where the protocol is invoked by someone acting autonomously, who is not under conditions of pressure, duress, temptation, intoxication, starvation, sleep-depravation etc. But they seem to rely on a situation where we grant the person invoking the protocol more authority than the person bound by it. The protocol is invoked by a 'reasonable' person for conditions where they foresee not acting reasonably. Odysseus protocols are examples of self-binding; the person bound by the protocol is bound on the sole-authority of the person who made it, and they are the very same person who is now bound by it.

Self-binding in perpetuity seems more extreme, however. It suggests that you will never be in a position to be better informed or more reasonable than at this moment. Yet we notice that institutions engage in such behaviour all the time. A constitution is a perpetual Odysseus protocol by a state on the future action of that state. Some constitutions allow for (often elaborate) procedures for amending the constitution, but even so, this is an instance of a government at one time binding future governments in perpetuity. The elaborate procedures for changing the constitution are expressly for the purpose of presenting future legislators choosing freely what laws to pass. Although this is the case of an institution binding itself, the future legislators are of course entirely different people. For this to make sense, we'd need to be sure that the generation of legislators were more reasonable than future generations would be. It's not always clear that this assumption holds in the case of actual constitutions. One consideration, particularly for democratic institutions, is that they are vulnerable to mood swings. The capacity for a shocking event to produce an over-reaction amongst law-makers is well known, particularly with respect to repealing civil-liberties in the face of a (perceived) external threat. There are perhaps specific types of law where giving civil-liberties the extra protection of belonging to the constitutional framework has been useful.

We've seen that promises require certain conditions, and that there are questions about whether it makes sense to bind future feelings and beliefs in the future, given the capacity for us to undergo transformative experiences. But we have also seen, in the form of deathbed promises and Odysseus protocols, that binding our own future action can be something it's useful to do.

CONCLUSIONS

We have reached the end of our journey. Let's reflect for a moment on some of the themes of this chapter, and of this book. One theme to attend to is of the open-endedness of questions of value. The passage of time compels us to reassess things, and a challenge for living is to live well in the face of the possibility that our actions may come to be a source of regret, or that our projects may never come to fruition.

When considering the different perspectives we sequentially take up, we can return to the topic of chapter 1. Do these changes of perspective represent a McTchange or a mere variation? Is what is changing time itself, or merely the information being considered?

One of the puzzles that the philosophy of time reveals is how the metaphysical relates to the ethical. We considered in chapters 5 and 6 the thought that the distinctively philosophical questions interact with the work of theoretical physicists. But those distinctively theoretical questions about whether there is McTchange and what gives rise to the asymmetries of records, intervention and affect relate to questions of how we decide, how we understand the past, and how we live.

Distressingly, the relation between the theoretical questions and the ethical ones isn't straightforward. It's not that if you accept one particular package in metaphysics you get a set of ethical results that you can act upon. Nor is it that if you've worked out how we ought to live you can reason back to what the metaphysics must be – at best you can reason as far as what you hope it can be.[10] But although it is not straightforward, there is a connection. These ethical questions are shaped by presuppositions about what time is. Hopefully now you have the resources to make your thought about those presuppositions explicit.

QUESTIONS FOR DISCUSSION

1. When can you tell if a life is well lived?
2. What kind of thing is it reasonable to commit to by swearing an oath?
3. What is the appropriate attitude to have towards lives you could have lived but didn't?

NOTES

1 Aristotle Nicomachean Ethics 1.X
2 Epicurus, quoted in Long and Sedley (1987) §24 A
3 https://www.poetryfoundation.org/poems/46565/ozymandias
4 Zhou Enlai was in fact responding to a question about the effects of the 1968 student riots, but people so liked the idea that the 1789 revolution was the topic that the misquote became widely believed.
5 In the old days we had proper nostalgia, not like the stuff you get nowadays.
6 See Pearson (2018) for a recent example of someone making this connection.
7 'A', 'B' and 'Γ' are the capital Greek letters alpha, beta, and gamma, respectively.
8 Jollimore 2011:119
9 One of the reasons studying philosophy can be a dangerous activity is its tendency to open up questions that had been treated as settled. It's best to entertain these ideas in a safe place with people you trust.
10 I discuss the role of hope further in Forbes (2023b).

FURTHER READING

O'Neill (1993) argues that our lives can go better after our deaths.

Banfi (2021) argues existential dread can't be made sense of if a static view of time is true.

Setiya (2016) examines why we feel a sense of loss of possibilities when we retrospect on our lives.

Lloyd (1993) argues that we should reject the need for a unified self to make sense of our lives over time.

GLOSSARY

'At-at' theory of change
Change is just a matter of things being one way *at* a time and another way *at* another time.

Affine structure
A geometrical structure that preserves straightness as well as topology.

Anosognosia
The phenomenon where something is presented in experience but does not get recognised.

A-series
A series of events based on their relation to the present.

Asymmetry of affect, the
The phenomenon where we have different attitudes based on whether something is future or past.

Asymmetry of intervention, the
The phenomenon where we can intervene on the present/future, but not on the past.

Asymmetry of records, the
The phenomenon where we have records of the past but not of the future.

Asymmetry of reference, the
The phenomenon where we can directly refer to something wholly in the past but not something that is wholly future.

A-theory
The view that we need an objective present to make sense of time.

Banana skin (time travel)
Whatever it is that prevents a grandfather paradox from arising in a timeline in which someone has the ability to cause themselves never to have existed, and attempts to do so.

Bias
A systematic tendency in favour of something rather than something else. Can be used in a mathematical sense (as in biased dice), or in a moral sense (a lack of impartiality).

B-series
A series ordered in terms of relations of before and after.

B-theory
The view that we can make sense of time with relations of before and after, but no objective present time.

Causal loop
A sequence of events such that some event is causally upstream of other events which are themselves causally upstream of it. A closed time-like curve would be an example of a causal loop.

Ceasing to be
The change of an object being destroyed.

Chaotic system
A system where small changes to the conditions of a system make a large difference to how the system evolves.

Closed time-like curve
A path through space–time where a journey is continually made in a later time-like direction (relative to the changing inertial frame of the traveller) that eventually intersects with a point in space–time 'earlier' in the journey.

Coming to be
The change of a new object forming.

Consistency (preference)
Consistent preferences are those that are stationary over time and invariant over time.

Continuous time
Time such that for all distinct times t_1 and t_2 there are uncountably many times between them.

C-series
A series ordered in terms that doesn't involve any appeal to time.

C-theory
The view that time doesn't require an objective present, or a fundamental distinction between earlier and later; both are imposed by our perspective on the world.

Dates
Time relationships specified in terms of the relations before, after, and simultaneous with.

Decision theory
The branch of philosophy that deals with questions about what makes a decision rational.

Dense time
Time such that for all distinct times t_1 and t_2, there are countably many times between them.

Deprivation account (death)
The view that death is bad because it deprives the deceased of something morally significant.

Determinism
The view that the state of a physical system at some time and the laws of nature entail the states of that system at other times. Often used to apply to the physical system that is the Universe.

Diachronic identity
Being one and the same thing over time.

Discount function (temporal)
A mathematical function that discounts the value of something based on some other property, in this case when it occurs.

Discrete time
Time such that if there is some time t_1 and some other time t_2 such that there are no times between t_1 and t_2.

Dominance
One option dominates another for an agent where the dominant option leaves an agent better off or no worse off than the dominated option. Strict dominance is where the dominant option always leaves the agent better off.

Dynamic view of time
A view of time according to which some change is McTchange.

Endurance
Persisting by being the proper subject of change, sometimes expressed as something being wholly present at each time it exists.

Entropic gradient, the
The increase of entropy in a system from the lowest entropy state to the highest entropy state, in accordance with the 2nd Law of Thermodynamics.

Entropy
A physical measure of disorder, understood as the number of ways a state can be achieved in a system. Notably used in the 2nd Law of Thermodynamics, which says the entropy of a closed system increases.

Episodic memory
Memory of episodes as having taken place, usually memories of what those episodes were like remembered from a particular point of view.

Error theory of change
A view that claims that there is no change, or that change is radically different from how it is ordinarily understood.

Euclidean Geometry
A geometrical model of physical space attributed to the Greek mathematician Euclid. It contains five postulates:

1. A circle of any radius can be drawn around any point.
2. A straight line can be drawn between any two points.

3. A straight line can be extended indefinitely.
4. All right angles are equal to each other.
5. If two straight lines intersect a third such that the sum of the inner angles on one side is less than two right angles, then the two lines, if extended far enough, must intersect on that side.

Exdurance
Persisting by being a momentary time-slice that stands in a causal-cum-similarity relation to other time-slices.

Expected utility
A numerical representation of the average goodness ('utility') of an outcome weighted by the likelihoods of the different possible outcomes.

Extensional account of temporal experience
An account of experience inspired by the writing of William James in which we experience an extended period of time including the present along with some of the recent past and some of the immediate future.

Factivity
Being a true representation or corresponding to the facts.

Fatalism
The view that the future is settled, and that this has bad consequences for the possibility or meaningfulness of human action.

Fixtures
Things that are not subject to choice.

Flow (experience)
An experience of time passing.

Fragmentalism about tense
The view that reality is irreducibly incoherent. There are fragments of reality that are coherent, but there's no way of having all the facts that make up reality form a coherent whole.

Galilean Relativity
The velocities of objects can be measured relative to an inertial frame.

General Theory of Relativity, the
A physical account of how space and time relate to, and are inseparable from, gravity.

Grandfather paradox
The paradox that a time traveller appears to have the ability to cause themselves never to have existed.

Growing Block, the
The view that the past exists and the future does not; reality gets bigger as things happen.

Hallucinations
Experiences where it appears that there is something, but there is nothing beyond the appearance.

Hedonism
The view that pleasure and pain are the only morally significant things.

Heisenberg's Uncertainty Principle
A principle in quantum theory according to which something's location and its momentum cannot both be precisely known, because attempting to measure one affects the other.

Hermeneutic
Involving interpretation.

History
A description of the past, or the project of providing that description.

Illusions
Cases of perception where the thing perceived appears in a way that is misleading.

Impermanence
(Pali 'anicca'; Sanskrit 'anitya') One of the three Buddhist marks of existence. All existing things are in a state of change from one form to another.

Indiscernibility of identicals
The principle that something must have all the same properties as itself. Equivalent to the claim that nothing can have inconsistent properties.

Inertial frame, an
A frame of reference used in physics treated as stationary for the purposes of measuring things moving relative to it.

Intransitive preferences
Preferences that fail to stand in transitive relations to one another. Illustrated in Figure 8.1.

Invariance (preference)
Invariant preferences are preferences for an outcome that a decision-maker values the same amount regardless of the distance of that outcome in time.

Lasting
Something not changing for a period of time.

Longtermism
The view that we should assess the utility of a decision based on its long-term consequences by not prioritising near-term consequences.

McTchange
Change over time that has no spatial equivalent.

Metric
A geometrical structure that preserves affine structure, distances and angles.

Money pump
A situation where money can be indefinitely extracted from someone as a result of intransitive preferences.

Moveable objective present (MOP)
A view of time travel in which there is an objective fact about what is present that time travel involves the relocation of.

Movement
Change in location of an object (or change in location of parts of an object).

Moving Spotlight, the
The view that the past present and future are all equally real, but the present is picked out as special in some way, as though there were a spotlight on it that moves as the present gets later and later.

Non-Enduring Claim of Buddhism
The claim by some Buddhists that we must reject endurance as an account of our own persistence through change.

Non-locality
A phenomenon in Quantum Theory where there seems to be no precise location for certain events, often described in terms of the 'entanglement' of quantum particles across arbitrarily large distances. Different interpretations of quantum theory explain the (widely experimentally confirmed) phenomenon of non-locality in different terms.

Not-Self
(Pali '*anatta*'; Sanskrit '*anatman*') One of the three Buddhist marks of existence. The denial that people have permanent unchanging essences.

Oath
A promise that is permanently binding, from which the swearer cannot be released.

Options
Things that can be chosen.

Perceptual experiences
Experiences that present the world as being a certain way, as contrasted with memories, anticipation, imagination and introspection.

Perdurance
Persisting by having different temporal parts at different times.

Persistence
Being the same thing through change over time.

Planck-length, the
The smallest measurable unit of distance (1.616255×10^{-35} m).

Planck-time
The amount of time it takes light to travel 1 Planck-length in a vacuum (5.391247×10^{-44} s).

Postmodernism
A philosophical movement that rejects the idea that there is coherent sense to be made out of things taken as a whole, and in particular a rejection of overarching metanarratives that describe history as having an overall point.

Presence in experience
The minimal experience of something being presented in experience.

Presentism
The view that only the present exists.

Qualitative change
Change in the qualities of an object.

Quantum Gravity
A theory combining the General Theory of Relativity and Quantum Theory to treat space–time as made up of smallest units called 'quanta'.

Quantum Theory
A theory of the nature of matter in the Universe according to which matter/energy are not infinitely divisible, but have smallest units called 'quanta'.

Radical Claim of Buddhism
The claim by some Buddhists that the way we ordinarily live/think needs to be overcome.

Reichenbachian simultaneity
The definition of simultaneity in the Special Theory of Relativity where the timing of a distant event is based on half the time it would take light to make a round trip relative to your local inertial frame. Illustrated in Figure 5.2.

Relativism about tense
The view that the facts that make up reality are real *relative* to different times. On this view, reality is composed of tensed facts, no time is privileged compared to others, and the world is a coherent one. It's just that whether some facts belong to reality is relative to what time it is.

Retentional account of temporal experience
An account of experience inspired by the writing of Edmund Husserl on which we experience the present as containing 'retentions' of the past, and 'protensions' (anticipations) of the future. Also known as a memory account.

Shrinking Block, the
The view that the future exists and the past does not exist; reality shrinks as time passes.

Shrinking Tree, the
The view that the past, present, and multiple possible futures are equally real. As those possible futures cease to be possible, they drop out of existence.

Static view of time
A view of time according to which all change is merely 'at–at' change.

Stationarity (preference)
Stationary preferences are preferences for outcomes that a decision-maker values just on the basis of how good/bad they are and the amount of time between them.

Stochastic system
A system which is not deterministic; the evolution of the system is chancy.

Succession
Something happening and then something else happening.

Symmetry
A logical property of relations. If x is the same as y, y is the same as x. The property of not being symmetric is asymmetry.

Temporal order
The relation of multiple events in terms of earlier or later.

Tense
A feature of language that locates events in time relative to a present time. Also a property of times involving presentness, pastness or futurity.

The Annals of St Gall
A medieval record of events in what is now southwestern Germany between 709 and 1059, comprising *Annales Alamannici* and the *Annales Sangallenses maiores*.

Theory of Relativity
The physical theory that space and time must be considered as part of the same four-dimensional manifold: space–time. The Special Theory of Relativity ignores the role of gravity, while the General Theory of Relativity includes the role of gravity.

Thermodynamics
The study of the transfer of heat. Much of what applies to heat also applies to transfers of energy and of information.

Time-reversal invariance
The property of not varying if the direction of time is reversed.

Topology
A geometrical structure that preserves intersections of lines, shapes being inside other shapes or outside them, and holes in shapes.

Transformative experiences
Experiences that significantly change the basis on which you assess the value of outcomes, by changing your ability to know and/or what you value.

Transitivity
A logical property of relations. If x is the same as y, and y is the same as z, then x is the same as z. The property of not being transitive is intransitivity.

Unity of agency, diachronic
The requirement that, in order to be able to act, agents must be unified over time.

Unity of agency, synchronic
The requirement that, in order to be able to act, agents must be unified at time.

Unsatisfactoriness

(Pali '*dukkha*'; Sanskrit '*duhkha*') One of the three Buddhist marks of existence. Unsatisfactoriness or suffering arises from a failure to accept the impermanence of all things.

Utility

A measure of goodness of outcomes. A utility function maps outcomes to values and the utilities are the values of those outcomes.

Wave-particle duality

A phenomenon in Quantum Theory in which energy/mass behaves in a wave-like manner under some conditions, and a particle-like manner under other conditions.

REFERENCES

Albert, David Z. (1992) *Quantum Mechanics and Experience*, London: Harvard University Press

——— (2000) *Time and Chance*, London: Harvard University Press

Aristotle *Nichomachean Ethics*, trans. Christopher Rowe (2002) Oxford: Oxford University Press

——— 'Metaphysics' in Jonathan Barnes (ed.) (1984) *The Complete Works of Aristotle*, Oxford: Princeton University Press

——— 'The Parts of Animals' in Jonathan Barnes (ed.) (1984) *The Complete Works of Aristotle*, Oxford: Princeton University Press

Augustine *Confessions*, trans. Thomas Williams (2019) Indianapolis: Hackett

Austen, Jane (1813/2003) *Pride and Prejudice*, London: Penguin

Austin, John Langshaw (1962) *How to Do Things with Words*, Oxford: Clarendon Press

Baldwin, James (1966) 'Unnameable Objects, Unspeakable Crimes', in The Editors of Ebony (ed.) *The White Problem in America*, Chicago: Johnson Publishing Company, pp. 173–181

Banfi, Luca (2021) 'Existential Dread and the B-theory of Time', *Synthese* (5–6): 1–18

Barbour, Julian (1999) *The End of Time*, Oxford: Oxford University Press

Barthes, Roland (1981/1967) 'The Discourse of History', trans. S. Bann, *Comparative Criticism* 3: 7–20

Baron, Sam; Miller, Kristie, and Tallant, Jonathan (2022) *Out of Time: A Philosophical Study of Timelessness*, Oxford: Oxford University Press

Baron, Sam; Latham, Andrew; Miller, Kristie, and Oh, Jordan (MS) 'Is Endurantism the Folk Friendly View of Persistence?'

Beebee, Helen (2000) 'The Non-Governing Conception of Laws of Nature', *Philosophy and Phenomenological Research* 61 (3): 571–594

Bennett, Christopher (2010). *What is This Thing Called Ethics?* London: Routledge

Bernstein, Sara (2017) 'Time Travel and the Movable Present', in John Keller (ed.), *Being, Freedom, and Method: Themes from the Philosophy of Peter van Inwagen*, Oxford: Oxford University Press, pp. 80–94

Bobzein, Susanne. (2021) *Determinism, Freedom, and Moral Responsibility*, Oxford: Oxford University Press

Bourne, Craig (2002) 'When Am I? A Tense Time for Some Tense Theorists?' *Australasian Journal of Philosophy* 80 (3): 359–371

―――― (2006) *A Future for Presentism*, Oxford: Oxford University Press

Braddon-Mitchell (2004) 'How Do we Know it Is Now Now?' *Analysis* 64 (3): 199–203

Briggs, R.A. and Forbes, G.A. (2012) 'The Real Truth about the Unreal Future', in K. Bennett and D. Zimmerman (eds) *Oxford Studies in Metaphysics* (Vol. 7), Oxford: Oxford University Press

Broad, C.D. (1923) *Scientific Thought*, London: Routledge and Keagan Paul

―――― (1938) *Examination of McTaggart's Philosophy Vol. II*, Cambridge: Cambridge University Press

―――― (1959) 'A Reply to my Critics', in P.A. Schlipp (ed.), *The Philosophy of C.D. Broad*, Tudor: New York Broad, pp. 711–830

Callender, Craig (2012) 'Time's Ontic Voltage', in Adrian Bardon (ed.), *The Future of the Philosophy of Time*, London, UK: Routledge, pp. 73–94

―――― (2017) *What Makes Time Special?* Oxford: Oxford University Press

―――― (2021) 'The Normative Standard for Future Discounting', *Australasian Philosophical Review* 5 (3): 227–253

Cantor, Georg (1891) 'Ueber eine elementare Frage der Mannigfaltigkeitslehre', *Jahresbericht der Deutschen Mathematiker-Vereinigung* 1: 75–78. English translation: Ewald, William B., ed. (1996) *From Immanuel Kant to David Hilbert: A Source Book in the Foundations of Mathematics, Volume 2.* Oxford University Press, pp. 920–922

Cameron, R. (2015) *The Moving Spotlight*, Oxford: Oxford University Press

Carpenter, Amber (2014) *Indian Buddhist Philosophy*, London: Routledge

Casati, R. and Torrengo, G. (2011) 'The Not So Incredible Shrinking Future', *Analysis* 71 (2):240–244

Collingwood, R.G. (1946/1994) *The Idea of History* (ed. J. Dussen), Oxford: Oxford University Press

Confucius (2003) *Analects: With Selections from Traditional Commentaries*, trans. Edward G. Slingerland Indianapolis: Hackett

Correia, Fabrice and Rosenkranz, Sven (2013) 'Living on the Brink, or Welcome Back, Growing Block!' *Oxford Studies in Metaphysics* 8: 333

―――― (2018) *Nothing to Come: A Defence of the Growing Block Theory of Time*, Cham, Switzerland: Springer Verlag

Dainton, Barry (2011) 'Time, Passage, and Immediate Experience', in C. Callender (ed.) *The Oxford Handbook of Philosophy of Time*, Oxford: Oxford University Press

——— (2022) 'Temporal Consciousness', *The Stanford Encyclopedia of Philosophy* (Summer 2022 Edition), Edward N. Zalta (ed.), URL = <https://plato.stanford.edu/archives/sum2022/entries/consciousness-temporal/>

Danto, Arthur (1985) *Narration and Knowledge*, Chichester: Columbia University Press

Dasti, Matthew R. and Bryant, Edwin F. (eds) (2013) *Free Will, Agency, and Selfhood in Indian Philosophy* Oxford: Oxford University Press

Davidson, Donald; McKinsey, J.C.C., and Suppes, Patrick, (1955) 'Outlines of a Formal Theory of Value, I', *Philosophy of Science* 22: 140–160

Day, Mark (2008). *The Philosophy of History: An Introduction*, Continuum

Deleuze, Gilles, and Guattari, Felix (1980/2004) *A Thousand Plateaus: Capitalism and Schizophrenia* (trans. Brian Massumi), Minneapolis, Minnesota: University of Minnesota Press

Deng, Natalja (2013a) 'Fine's McTaggart, Temporal Passage, and the A versus B Debate', *Ratio* 26 (1): 19–34

Deng, N. (2013b) 'On Explaining Why Time Seems to Pass', *Southern Journal of Philosophy* 51 (3): 367–382

Dixon, F.M.A. (2022) *The Little House on Everywhere Street*, Raleigh, North Carolina: Regal House Publishing

Dowker, Faye (2014) 'The Birth of Spacetime Atoms as the Passage of Time', *Annals of the New York Academy of Sciences* 1326: 18–25

Effingham, Nikk (2020) *Time Travel: Probability and Impossibility*, Oxford: Oxford University Press

Eliot, T.S. (1944) *Four Quartets*, London: Faber and Faber

Fernandes, Alison Sutton (2019) 'Does the Temporal Asymmetry of Value Support a Tensed Metaphysics?' *Synthese* 3999–4016

Fine, Kit (2005) 'Tense and Reality', in *Modality and Tense*, Oxford: Oxford University Press, pp. 261–320

Forbes, Graeme A. (2016) 'The Growing Block's Past Problems', *Philosophical Studies* 173(3): 699–709

——— (2023a) 'The 2D Past', in K. Jaszczolt (ed.) *Understanding Human Time*, Oxford: Oxford University Press

——— (2023b) 'Critical Commonsensism in Contemporary Metaphysics', in R. Talisse, P. Reyes Cardenas and D. Herbert (eds) *Pragmatic Reason*, London: Routledge

Frischhut, Akiko M. (2015) 'What Experience Cannot Teach Us About Time', *Topoi* 34 (1):143–155

Gale, R.M. (1968) *The Philosophy of Time*, London: Macmillan

Gallie, Walter B. (1964) *Philosophy and the Historical Understanding*, New York: Schocken Books

Geach, P.T. (1969) *God and the Soul*, London: Routledge and Keagan Paul

Gestmin SGPS SA v Credit Suisse (UK) Ltd & Anor [2013] EWHC 3560 (Comm)

Godfrey-Smith, P. (2018) *Other Minds: The Octopus and the Evolution of Intelligent Life*, London: William Collins

Greene, Preston, and Sullivan, Meghan (2015) 'Against Time Bias', *Ethics* 125 (4): 947–970

Grünbaum, Adolf (1986) *Modern Science and Zeno's Paradoxes*, London: George and Allen Unwin

Grush, R. (2007) 'Time & Experience', in *Philosophie der Zeit*, T. Müller (ed.), Frankfurt: Klosterman

Haack, Susan (1998) *Manifesto of a Passionate Moderate*, Chicago, Illinois: University of Chicago Press

Hare, Caspar (2018) *On Myself and Other, Less Important Subjects*, Oxford: Princeton University Press

Harman, E. (2009) '"I'll be glad I did it" Reasoning and the Significance of Future Desires', *Philosophical Perspectives* 23: 177–199

Haslanger, S. (2003) 'Persistence Through Time', in D. Zimmerman and M. Loux (eds) *The Oxford Handbook in Metaphysics*, Oxford: Oxford University Press, pp. 315–354

Hawley, Katherine (2001) *How Things Persist*, Oxford: Oxford University Press

—— (2020) *How to Be Trustworthy*, Oxford: Oxford University Press

Hoerl, Christoph (2013) 'A Succession of Feelings, in and of Itself, is not a Feeling of Succession', *Mind* 122 (486): 373–417

—— (2014) 'Do we (Seem to) Perceive Passage?' *Philosophical Explorations* 17 (2): 188–202

Homer *The Odyssey* Trans. Anthony Verity (2017) Oxford University Press

Horwich. P. (1987) *Asymmetries in Time*, London: MIT Press

Hume, David (1999) *Enquiry Concerning Human Understanding*, Oxford: Oxford University Press

Ingram, D. (2016) 'The Virtues of Thisness Presentism', *Philosophical Studies* 173: 2867–2888

—— (2018) *Thisness Presentism*, London: Routledge

Johnston, Mark (1984) *Particulars and Persistence*, Dissertation, Princeton University

—— (2011) *Surviving Death*, Oxford: Princeton University Press

Jollimore, T. (2011) *Love's Vision*, Oxford: Princeton University Press

Kane, Gordon L. (2017) *String Theory and the Real World*, Bristol: IOP Publishing

Kayani, A.; King, M.J. and Fleiter, J.J. (2012) 'Fatalism and its Implications for Risky Road Use and Receptiveness to Safety Messages: A Qualitative Investigation in Pakistan', *Health Education Research* 27 (6): 1043–1054, https://doi.org/10.1093/her/cys096

Knoke, Thomas; Gosling, Elizabeth, and Paul, Carola (2020) 'Use and Misuse of the Net Present Value in Environmental Studies', *Ecological Economics* 174 (106664): 1–15

Korsgaard, Christine M. (1989) 'Personal Identity and the Unity of Agency', *Philosophy and Public Affairs* 18 (2): 101–132

Kroll, Nicky (2020) 'Passing Time', *Erkenntnis* 85 (1): 255–268

Lam, Derek (2021) 'The Phenomenology and Metaphysics of the Open Future', *Philosophical Studies* 178 (12): 3895–3921

Le Poidevin, Robin (2002) 'Zeno's Arrow and the Significance of the Present', *Royal Institute of Philosophy Supplement* 50: 57–72

Lear, Jonathan (1981) 'A Note on Zeno's Arrow', *Phronesis* 26 (2): 91–104

Lenman, James (2000) 'Consequentialism and Cluelessness', *Philosophy and Public Affairs* 29 (4): 342–370

Lewis, David K. (1976) 'The Paradoxes of Time Travel', *American Philosophical Quarterly* 13 (2):145–152

—— (1981) 'Are we Free to Break the Laws?', *Theoria* 47 (3): 113–121

—— (1986) *On the Plurality of Worlds*, Oxford: Blackwell

Lisvane, Lord (2018, January 30) *HL* European Union (Withdrawal) Bill Debate, 30 January 2018, vol788 c1492. https://hansard.parliament.uk/Lords/2018-01-30/debates/DEF7D976-EE5D-4150-BC6D-2F2C928719C5/EuropeanUnion(Withdrawal)Bill

Lloyd, Daniel (2002) 'Functional MRI and the Study of Human Consciousness', *Journal of Cognitve Neuroscience* 14 (6): 818–831

Lloyd, Genevieve (1993) *Being in Time: Selves and Narrators in Philosophy and Literature*, London: Routledge

Locke, John, (1690/2004) *An Essay Concerning Humane Understanding*, Roger Woolhouse (ed.) London: Penguin

Long, A.A., and Sedley, D.N. (1987) *The Hellenistic Philosophers*, Cambridge: Cambridge University Press

Lyotard, Jean-François (1979/2001) *The Postmodern Condition: A Report on Knowledge*, trans. G. Bennington and B. Massumi, Manchester: Manchester University Press

MacAskill, William (2022) *What We Owe The Future*, London: Oneworld Publications

McCall, Storrs (1994) A Model of the Universe. *Philosophical Quarterly* 47 (186): 113–115

McDaniel, Kris (2007) 'Distance and Discrete Space', *Synthese* 155 (1): 157–162

McInerney, P.K. (1991) *Time and Experience*, Philadelphia: Temple University Press

MacIntyre, Alastair (2006) *Ethics and Politics: Selected Essays* (Vol. 2), Cambridge: Cambridge University Press

Markosian, Ned (2004) 'A Defense of Presentism', in D. Zimmerman (ed.) *Oxford Studies in Metaphysics* (Vol. 1), Oxford: Oxford University Press

Maudlin, T. (2002) 'Remarks on the Passing of Time', *Proceedings of the Aristotelian Society* 102: 259–274

Maudlin, T. (2012) *Philosophy of Physics: Space and Time*, Oxford: Princeton University Press

Mellor, D.H. (1998) *Real Time II*, London: Routledge

Merleau-Ponty, Maurice (1945/2004) *The Phenomenology of Perception*, London: Routledge

Miller, Kristie (2017) 'A Taxonomy of Views about Time in Buddhist and Western Philosophy', *Philosophy East and West* 67 (3): 763–782

Miller, Kristie (2018) 'The New Growing Block Theory vs Presentism', *Inquiry: An Interdisciplinary Journal of Philosophy* 61 (3): 223–251

Miller, Kristie (2019) 'The Cresting Wave: A New Moving Spotlight Theory', *Canadian Journal of Philosophy* 49 (1): 94–122

Mink, Louis (1970) 'History and Fiction as Modes of Comprehension', *New Literary History* 1: 541–558

Mischel, W.; Shoda, Y., and Rodriguez M. I. (1989) 'Delay of Gratification in Children', *Science* 244: 933–938

Nagel, Thomas (1971) 'Brain Bisection and the Unity of Consciousness', *Synthese* 22: 396–413

––––– (1979) *Mortal Questions*, Cambridge: Cambridge University Press

––––– (1986) *The View From Nowhere*, Oxford: Oxford University Press

Niffenegger, Audrey (2003) *The Time Traveler's Wife*, San Fransisco, California: McAdam/Cage

Norton, John D. (2015). The Burning Fuse Model of Unbecoming in Time, *Studies in History and Philosophy of Science Part B: Studies in History and Philosophy of Modern Physics* 52 (Part A): 103–105

O'Neill, J. (1993) 'Future Generations: Present Harms', *Philosophy* 68 (263): 35–51

Olson, Eric T. (2009) 'The Rate of Time's Passage', *Analysis* 69 (1): 3–9

Owen, G.E.L. (1958) 'Zeno and the Mathematicians', *Proceedings of the Aristotelian Society* 58: 199–222

Parfit, Derek (1984) *Reasons and Persons*, Oxford: Oxford University Press

Paul, L.A. (2015) 'What You Can't Expect When You're Expecting', *Res Philosophica* 92 (2): 1–23

––––– (2017) 'The Subjectively Enduring Self', in Ian Phillips (ed.), *Routledge Handbook of the Philosophy of Temporal Experience*, London and New York: Routledge

Pearson, Olley (2018) 'Appropriate Emotions and the Metaphysics of Time', *Philosophical Studies* 175 (8): 1945–1961

Peirce, Charles Sanders (1935) *The Collected Papers of Charles Sanders Peirce*, ed. Charles Hartshorne and Paul Weiss, 8 vols, Cambridge MA: Harvard University Press

Perrett, Roy W. (2016) *An Introduction to Indian Philosophy*, Cambridge: Cambridge University Press

Pettigrew, Richard (2019) *Choosing for Changing Selves*, Oxford, UK: Oxford University Press

Phillips, Ian (2014) 'The Temporal Structure of Experience', in D. Lloyd and V. Arstila, *Subjective Time*, London: MIT Press, pp. 139–159

Power, Sean Enda (2018) *Philosophy of Time and Perceptual Experience*, London: Routledge

Pratchett, Terry (1992) *Lords and Ladies*, London: Corgi

Price, Huw (1996) *Time's Arrow and Archimedes Point*, Oxford: Oxford University Press

Prosser, Simon (2011) 'Why Does Time Seem to Pass?' *Philosophy and Phenomenological Research* 85 (1): 92–116

Prosser, Simon (2016) *Experiencing Time*, Oxford, UK: Oxford University Press

Putnam, Hilary (1967) 'Time and Physical Geometry', *Journal of Philosophy* 64 (8): 240–247

Ramsey, F.P. (1928) 'A Mathematical Theory of Saving', *Economic Journal* 38 (4): 543–559

Raphael, D. D. (1969) *British Moralists*, 2 vols, London: Oxford, Clarendon Press

Raven, M.J. (2011) 'Can Time Pass at a Rate of 1 Second per Second', *Australasian Journal of Philosophy* 89: 459–465

Rennick, Stephanie (2015) 'Things Mere Mortals *Can* Do, But Philosophers Can't', *Analysis* 75 (1): 22–26, https://doi.org/10.1093/analys/anu097

Rovelli, Carlo, and Vidotto, Francesca (2015) *Covariant Loop Quantum Gravity*, Cambridge: Cambridge University Press

Russell, Bertrand (1903) *The Principles of Mathematics*, Cambridge: Cambridge University Press

Sainsbury, Richard Mark (2009) *Paradoxes* (3rd edn), Cambridge: Cambridge University Press

Sacks, Oliver (1970) *Migraine*, Berkeley: University of California Press

Salmon, Wesley (1980) *Space, Time, and Motion*, Minneapolis: University of Minnesota Press

Sanford, David H. (1968) 'McTaggart on Time', *Philosophy* 43 (166): 371–378

Segal, Peter (dir.) (1994) *Naked Gun 33 1/3: The Final Insult*, Hollywood, California: Paramount

Setiya, Kieran (2014) 'The Ethics of Existence', *Philosophical Perspectives* 28 (1): 291–301

——— (2016) 'Retrospection', *Philosophers' Imprint* 16 (15): 1–15

——— (2022) *Life is Hard*, London: Hutchison Heinemann

Shardlow, Jack; Lee, Ruth; Hoerl, Christoph; McCormack, Teresa; Burns, Patrick, and Fernandes, Alison S. (2021) 'Exploring People's Beliefs about the Experience of Time', *Synthese* 198 (11): 10709–10731

Sider, T. (2001) *Fourdimensionalism*, Oxford: Oxford University Press

Sklar, Lawrence (1977) S*pace Time and Spacetime*, London: University of California Press

Smolin, Lee (2009) 'Generic Predictions of Quantum Theories of Gravity', in Daniele Oriti (ed.), *Approaches to Quantum Gravity: Toward a New Understanding of Space, Time and Matter*, Cambridge: Cambridge University Press, pp. 548–570

Sorabji, Richard (1983) *Time, Creation, and the Continuum: Theories in Antiquity and the Early Middle Ages*, Chicago: University of Chicago Press

Sullivan, Meghan (2018) *Time Biases: A Theory of Rational Planning and Personal Persistence*, Oxford, UK: Oxford University Press

Tallant, Jonathan Charles (2014) 'Defining Existence Presentism', *Erkenntnis* 79 (S3): 479–501

Todd, Patrick (2021) *The Open Future: Why All Future Contingents Are False*, Oxford: Oxford: University Press

Tooley, Michael (1998) *Time, Tense, and Causation*, Oxford: Oxford University Press

Torrengo, Giuliano (2017) 'Feeling the Passing of Time', *Journal of Philosophy* 114 (4): 165–188

Thomson, G., and Macpherson, F. (November 2020) 'Rotating Snakes Illusion', in F. Macpherson (ed.), *The Illusions Index*. Retrieved from https://www.illusionsindex.org/i/22-rotating-snakes

Thomson, James (1954) 'Tasks and Supertasks', *Analysis* 15 (1): 1–13

Valberg, J.J. (2012) 'The Irrevocability of Being', *Philosophy* 87 (339): 65–77

Van Gelder, T. (1996) 'Wooden Iron? Husserlian Phenomenology Meets Cognitive Science', *Electronic Journal of Analytic Philosophy* 4

Van Inwagen, Peter, (1983) '*An Essay on Free Will*', Oxford: Oxford University Press

——— (2010) 'Changing the Past', *Oxford Studies in Metaphysics* 5: 3–40

Varela, F. (1999) 'Present-time Consciousness', *Journal of Consciousness Studies* 6 (2–3): 111–140

Velleman, J. David. (2006) 'So It Goes', *The Amherst Lecture in Philosophy* 1: 1–23. http://www.amherstlecture.org/velleman2006/

Wasserman, Ryan (2017). *Paradoxes of Time Travel*, Oxford, UK: Oxford University Press

Wells, H.G. (1895) *The Time Machine*, London: William Heinemann

Wheeler, John Archibald (1978) 'The "Past" and the "Delayed-Choice" Double-Slit Experiment', in A. R. Marlow (ed.), *Mathematical Foundations of Quantum Theory*, Academic Press, pp. 9–48

White, Hayden (1980) 'The Value of Narrativity in the Representation of Reality', *Critical Inquiry* 7 (1): 5–27

Wittgenstein, Ludwig (1922/1961) *Tractatus Logico-Philosophicus*, trans. D.F. Pears and B.F. McGuinness, London: Routledge

Wolf, Susan (1986) 'Self-Interest and Interest in Selves', *Ethics* 96 (4): 704–720

Woodward, J. (2005) *Making Things Happen*, Oxford: Oxford University Press

Zagzebski, L.T. (2015) 'Omniscience and the Arrow of Time', in J.M. Fischer and P. Todd (eds) *Freedom, Fatalism, and Foreknowledge*, Oxford: Oxford University Press

Zahavi, Daniel (2007) 'Perception of Duration Presupposes Duration of Perception – or Does it? Husserl and Dainton on Time', *International Journal of Philosophical Studies* 15 (3): 453–471

Zhou Enlai. In Ratcliffe S. (Ed.), *Oxford Essential Quotations*, Oxford University Press. Retrieved 24 Dec. 2022, from https://www.oxfordreference.com/view/10.1093/acref/9780191826719.001.0001/q-oro-ed4-00018657

INDEX

Printed in the United States
by Baker & Taylor Publisher Services